yearbook
of
INDIAN POETRY IN ENGLISH
2021

EDITORS

SUKRITA PAUL KUMAR
VINITA AGRAWAL

Hawakal
PUBLISHERS

New Delhi | Calcutta

HAWAKAL
New Delhi | Calcutta

HAWAKAL PUBLISHERS

70 B/9 Amritpuri, East of Kailash, New Delhi 65
33/1/2 K B Sarani, Mall Road, Calcutta 80

info@hawakal.com
www.hawakal.com

Cover designed by Bitan Chakraborty

First edition (paperback) June 2022

ISBN: 978-93-91431-69-3

Price: INR 650 | USD 22.99

INTRODUCTION

It's been vastly fulfilling to carry forward the task of putting together the second edition of the *Yearbook of Indian Poetry in English*. This year, i.e. for the *Yearbook* 2021, we've taken a practical decision to consider poems calendar wise. This year (because of the submission period announced last year) it also entails reading poems published in November and December 2020. However, it means that next year onwards, we will read and include exactly twelve months' worth of quality poetry as opposed to the fourteen months that we needed to look at this year.

Like the previous year, this time too there was an overwhelming response to our call for submissions. The *Yearbook of Indian Poetry in English* 2021 celebrates and speaks for the creative engagement of the young and the veterans with both, the sensitive responses to life's varied experiences as well as their skilfully crafted articulation of issues that warrant attention. This year we received poems that reflected the diversity of concerns as they traversed across regions, gender, caste and style. Reading them was like travelling through the length and breadth of the country and abroad, thanks to the submissions by Indian diaspora. That's the thing about poetry — it allows you to dwell in many different locales without actually moving physically. And more importantly, it allows you to enter domains not ordinarily visible. Poetry helps unravel and map an inner terrain effectively, stripping away superficial veneers and allowing for fresh dimensions of truth to be introduced.

We, as editors, had the task of sieving the more stirring and insightful poems from amongst 700 poems either submitted or nominated for the second edition of the *Yearbook*. Following the practice evolved last year, we put together a jury of poets who graciously agreed to help us make a selection of 142 poems through an anonymous review. We are deeply grateful to the jury for conscientiously and perceptively, picking the poems of their choice during the review process, from the long list sent to them. The collation of the final selection was done by the editors and what is presented in this volume is a selection as objective as we could manage.

We celebrate a collective choice of poems for the *Yearbook* 2021. We must hasten to mention here that editors of several journals contributed to the worth of the *Yearbook* by nominating outstanding poems published by them during the specified period of submission. All efforts were made not to miss out on these quality poems. Despite all our efforts, it is possible that some voices may still have been left out — either because they did not submit or because their work was not published in the stipulated time frame. This year too the focus remained on the poem and not the poet, which is why the review was once again, anonymous. This is the very process that happily threw up some new and young poets alongside many illustrious names. We hope that those not in the book this year, will make it next year, ready for the same kind of rigorous process. The astute and keen eye of each of the following members of the jury is appreciated with warm and plentiful thanks: Sampurna Chattarji, Mustansir Dalvi, Gayatri Majumdar, Rishi Dastidar, Maaz Bin Bilal. What ultimately brings the project to fruition is undoubtedly the enthusiastic support of the publishers in *Hawakal*. We would particularly like to acknowledge the challenges faced by the publishers in compiling the concrete poems in the anthology. They devised some innovative methods (inserting the poem as a photo, for example) to incorporate these poems in the *Yearbook*. Thank you Kiriti Sengupta, Bitan Chakraborty and their entire team.

This time around we have a new section in the *Yearbook*, titled Beacon Lights — where we showcase one published poem each, written by our senior, respected poets. They are in their eighties and nineties yet they belt out amazing poetry that is published either as a book or as part of a print or online journal. They do us proud which is why we would like to honour these stalwarts by dedicating a special section to them. We wish to reiterate here that the essential vision behind the *Yearbook* series is to archive and present quality Indian poetry published each year. The plethora of poetry in English being written, published and showcased is so overbearing — spread as it is over multitudinous journals (print and online) and books, national and international, that the task of critical appreciation becomes challenging. For the identification of major tradition(s) or even prominent trends in Indian poetry in English, the *Yearbook* may serve as an important support material produced by a collective of poets themselves. By no means is there an intention to encourage a spirit of juvenile competition in poetry, but it does alert one to pay heed to "quality" in the writing and reading of poetry. We hope that readers and scholars will find this to be an important and useful reference point to discern the ever-evolving aesthetics in this domain. The *Yearbook* hopes to facilitate a study of the changing dynamics of aesthetics demonstrated year after year. Each volume captures the contemporary as well as important historical and socio-political phenomena, notwithstanding the existential angst of the poet. This year we've taken a conscious decision to include only one poem per poet. This was done to broaden the gates for more poems and more names to make it to the stronghold of the *Yearbook*.

Understandably, the first *Yearbook* recorded an emphatic consciousness of the pandemic and the virus that took away so many lives. The plight of migrant labour, economic crunch, death consciousness and the long lock-downs shook people out of complacency. All of this was, in a natural manner, inscribed into the poems of many poets, at times directly and sometimes incipiently. This year, we observed a shift of attention in that the poetic sensibilities internalised the experiences of an ongoing pandemic on the one hand and engaged with on-the-ground experiences of life on the other. There was also considerable projection of a philosophic meandering on these matters. The following lines from different poems, for instance, make one confront a strange and confounding complexity of human existence: "*there is a truth hidden in every lie*", "*turn dream into stone*", "*eating an apple is eating the world*", "*no rafu of the heart*", "*what if we are dead already*", "*I carry my uterus in a suitcase*". When a poet says "*Writing isn't everything*", it perhaps ironically, indicates how in fact writing is everything. Yet another poet declares "*There is no country for writers*" and making a case for truth, laments that "*writing has become fake...*"

The treatment to the experience of both bilingualism and language itself, in several poems this year, projects a kind of spontaneous and unaffected expression rather than a self-conscious use of the English language for creative writing. However, in a poem such as "Foreign Language", the poet bemoans: "my languages my identity crossbred and crossed". Interestingly in another poem the word "khair" from Urdu becomes the poem's main subject and the translator's tension between English and Urdu is pronounced in a nuanced style. In yet another poem, Urdu is the focus of the poem. Then there is that evocative line in a poem: "Konkani slipped into my English like fat roaches".

While the multiplicity of languages amongst Indian poets is a great asset and a rich resource, there can also be a rather uncomfortable power struggle and friction between them. A healthy dialogue and negotiation between languages is what can strike a harmonious chord of accommodation rather than strife: "...*our curry laden tongues*" and "*spiced mouths*" can then lead to "*rolling syllables like pebbles*". Instead of clashing with each other, a poet articulates how "*the needle of my tongue*" sews the unspoken "*with the thread of the language/ into the fabric of our conversation*". The *Yearbook* offers a variety of perceptive and poetic formulations of the meaning of language. One of the poems courageously calls out to Wittgenstein to redefine language.

In the context of instabilities and uncertainties experienced acutely in contemporary life, it is not surprising that many poems in the *Yearbook* emerge creatively from a special focus on home, house, identity, roots and indeed as mentioned above, the question of language which is also deeply linked with the idea of homing. To our pleasant surprise, this volume has a large number of poems that suggest another kind of need for familial continuity, respect for relatedness and warm reassurance through poets invoking grandfathers, grandmothers and lineage in different ways in their poems. "*Grandma...was the woman closest/to the sun...*", in another poem there is this line: "*the tree growing out of grandfather's body, I saw roots down his toes*", and in yet another poem, the grandfather's caste-marks and dark skin are highlighted, invoking lineage.

With mythology living so vibrantly amidst our cultural context, mythological figures constantly become reference points for poets and writers to reimagine the established meanings with fresh ones. In this volume, whether it is the story of Galava and Madhavi in their earlier setting, Ahalya, or Ashwatthama carrying the wound in his forehead into the present day world, these poems accord an opportunity to re-examine and re-interpret mythology. Imaginative literary recreations sometimes revoke earlier stories that may be regressive or irrelevant. Sometimes an irreverent approach to the established frames becomes imperative to deconstruct rigid stereotypes for new perspectives to be explored. Who else but poets can undertake such a task?

There is a presence of diverse religious affiliations and a display of a fascinating variety of cuisine co-existing in parallel on the Indian landscape in this volume, thus adding to the overall experience of cultural diversity. What is also to be noted, however, is the use of the metaphor of *"tunnels between our houses"* facilitating easy connections. In fact animals, trees, places and objects seem to exist in an integrated way in this world of poetry accommodating even technology and new modes of communication. This inclusive world has no place for narrow bigotry or propaganda. Instead there is empathy, harmony, love and concern for the hungry and the deprived, for the vanishing frogs of Malabar, for the angst of those in exile, for those existing on the margins of society seeking social justice. In fact, there runs a spirit of questioning the status quo in many poems, making room for change so that *"hunger stones"* can make one weep, and love songs do not remain silenced.

When *"the forest will come to us"* or *"the earth whispers her secrets"*, and when a ghazal gets written for Covid-19 rather than on the beauty of the beloved, that's when one realises how humanity is calling out for a paradigm shift from some set perspectives in life. Nothing, after all, can be taken for granted. From the content in the poems to the style and form of the poems, poets are moving on actively to also deliberating on the use of space for the writing of their poems. When the poem on a temple spreads on the page visually, or the dance of the flamingo becomes a treat for the eyes as the architect of the poem uses words to paint the dance, it is fascinating to observe how "concrete poems" make meaning differently. The current *Yearbook* has a few such poems. It is hoped that literary critics will enjoy these poems and appreciate the diligence that goes into creating such work.

This edition of the *Yearbook* is also embedded with concerted poems on imperialism, gender (as always!), mental health, childhood traumas, upbringing, Earth, climate change, birds, mining, prostitutes, racism, sensuality and spirituality. Also, and this is a somewhat poignant point, the *Yearbook* has automatically become an ode to so many journals that have closed down in the present days. It's heartbreaking when a journal closes shop, especially if it is for economic reasons and pandemic dictates. It gives us warm satisfaction to realise that though some of the publications cited in this *Yearbook* are not be in operation anymore they get archived forever in the pages of the *Yearbook*.

The making of the *Yearbook of Indian Poetry in English 2021,* to our joy, has turned out to be a gorgeous potpourri of fragrances and flavours from different parts of the country and beyond, for readers to savour and join the chorus with their own instruments of creativity.

Sukrita and Vinita
June 2022

In Gratitude

The project of the *Yearbook* is a marathon venture made possible by a collective effort and commitment of people passionate about poetry. But for the spirit of pooling their individual expertise, time and labour, and gratis at that, the *Yearbook* would not happen.

To start with, we are extremely grateful to our Review Committee members, who conscientiously and with utmost grace, respected the anonymity of the poems submitted to them, and made their selections individually: Gayatri Majumdar, Maaz bin Bilal, Mustansir Dalvi, Rishi Dastidar and Sampurna Chattarji. Some of the our committee members were grappling with health issues, others were reading for well known poetry prizes yet they, very kindly, spared time to make their selections for the *Yearbook* and also kept to the deadlines.

We would also like to record our appreciation of the editors of several poetry journals, like *Poetry at Sangam*, *The Bombay Literary Magazine* and *EKL Review* for nominating quality poems of their choice published in the stipulated period, for this edition of the *Yearbook*.

Some distinguished poets, friends of the *Yearbook*, also helped in scouting for poems that merited attention and consideration for the *Yearbook*. Their pointers, particularly to the poetry of the Indian diaspora, which was painstakingly compiled for us, went through the selection process as per the norm. Thank you very much Shikha Malaviya and Satya Dash for your efforts and time for identifying good poetry.

A big thank you to Kiriti Sengupta, Bitan Chakraborty and the team at *Hawakal* for publishing the second volume of the *Yearbook* with as much warmth and enthusiasm as they did the first one.

We are thankful also to each and every single poet who submitted his/her precious work to the *Yearbook*. It is your memorable work that lends worth to this anthology. We are appreciative to have an even larger number of submissions this year in comparison to the previous edition. It is heartening to see more and more people, young and old, writing and engaging with poetry. We believe and hope that the number will keep growing and that the *Yearbook* will help in creating discerning readers for good poetry.

Sukrita Paul Kumar and Vinita Agrawal

CONTENTS

ABHAY K.
Exile

I measure my days
weeks, months, and years

A year is one third
of exile from the motherland.

First published in *Chipmunk*, India, June 2021

ABHISHEK ANICCA
Spine

I grew a spine at birth
carrying its imperfections
with pride
                 and you called me shame

I fostered a twisted column
of bones on my lips
with style
                 and you called me bitterness

I wore hunchbacks like a crown
reclaiming my beauty
with stride
                 and you called me monstrosity

My spine disappeared one day
and I started speaking
with guile
                 and you called me normal

First published in *Nether Quarterly*, Vol 2, Issue 2, Dec 2020

ACHITA KHARE
Poem Do Pyaza

I have stopped writing poems
Poems when written, are unyielding
Unyielding since they rock paper-chair like an old maid
A maid who sulks, frowns, and sings songs of antiquity
Antiquity with romance, but lack contemporary touch
Touch - right! That's what my poems need
Need skillful carving on a chopping board not edit table
Table on which it will be marinated by coarse fingers
Fingers which can touch and tell sugar and spices
Spices that add adventure for my eyes
Eyes which are now a wok
Wok where my poem will crackle when tossed
Tossed, or on a steamboat where they will bake slowly
Slowly, slowly will they acquire a crust, golden and crisp
Crisp like the autumn wind which vehemently blows
Blows your mind such a poem I will keep
Keep for your palate to savor
Savor a poem that I have not written
But, cooked

First published in *Gulmohar Quarterly*, Issue 2, June 2021

ADITHYA PATIL
Presets

Pick an hour:
Say the invigorating 6 pm dusk.
Pick a room:
Say the one farthest from the kitchen.
Clean its walls of poster.
On a square stand, by the sill
Fill a glass bowl with
The nakedness
Of shaved almonds.
For fondling,
Fill another with bald pebbles.
Arrange female chatter
But make sure it's distant,
Muffled if possible.
Drag the armchair across the floor
To before the silent window,
And so, create
The possibility of reflection.
When the air is ready and all has been set—

Enter Grandfather

First published in *Muse India*, Issue 95, Jan-Feb 2021

ADITYA SHANKAR
How to Read a Tree

Birds are golfers of heaven. They swing their
Club-like wings and score their birdie and par
In treetop nests. A tree is a vertical golf course,
Says the snake that gobbles up the egg. And a
Grassland of the highest branches—the Giraffe.
Watch closely. You can spot the Garibaldi beard
Of their stooping caddies, buzz the Bees. Human
Sighting of trees is the wrong side of an arena,
The gloomy lower of the green turf. Their poets
Stare at the underside and pine about seasons,
Foliage, solitude, and thorns. But a tree is the
Hardened cable of an elevator. In a netherworld
Of downswing, they maintain heavens of glee.
Beneath ecstasies and pleasures, we operate
Among seasoned roots and neurons of pain.

First published in *The International Zine Project*, Paris, Feb 2021

AFSAR MOHAMMAD
speaking from the street
for Lawrence Ferlinghetti who opened my eyes to a wave of urban/street idiom

1
s t r a y
dogs, orphaned cats
and then the people
walking dead
orshrunken on
some corner of the street.

screaming
ranting
and then wording.

2

eating, speaking
then jaywalking or
running wildly across
the roads.

These streets—

forever haunted by burning souls
that
never make a full sentence.

3
short lines on the

                              left margins

moving across a page
breaking into something
either to shout or howl
i read the empty spaces
as they keep crying their eyes out.

4
now imagine
a blood -smeared page

just guess it blends
with a stream of endless sweat
flowing restlessly from somewhere.

then see
a person or his gray trace
wakes up abruptly
to dream another dream
orphaned or abandoned
forever
un/
knowingly.

First published in *Beltway Poetry Quarterly*, Nov 2021

AJAY KUMAR
touchscream

diwali outside, & names smoke on my tongue
with the taste of burning diyas / in the TV's

glitching glow the blue chips packet is passed
around, the remote has a coat of masala magic

from our fingers / with a touch, I harvest red
notification blossoms on green whatsapp boughs

watch the single tick split into two, then turn
blue under the dotted shade of typing, online

typing, last seen, typing… click on clickbaits
to be proven right / like a worm in the damp

soil of the internet, hooked onto a promise of
water, however salty, only to come undone in

an algorithm of annuli / scroll thumbnails on
pornsites, looking for something the shape of

us / but not clicking on it, guilted by what I am
looking for / when a rare torrent finds a firm

seed, I feel the world might just get along sharing
touchscreen dreams from broken echochambers

in the 3am heat, a hum through a flame of clapping
hands becomes a hymn / apocalyptically lit blue

packets of petrol pumps dot my dream like masala
magic fireflies alighting on the branches of a dark

country creeping north / I wake up shooting pebbles
across eddying shallows of my mind to roiling blues

of my body & trace its descent into the phosphorous
dark while being kneedeep in it myself / I wake up

under a blue blanket patterned with leaves fleshing
peach at the tips, burned by fireworks of yesterday

First published in *The Bombay Literary Magazine*, Aug 2021
Nominated by *The Bombay Literary Magazine*

AEKTA KHUBCHANDANI
True or False

We talk too many languages at home, one louder than the other. It's impossible to trap a jugnu in a jar. Phulkari dupattas are better than lucknawi. I remain unscathed from the childhood I've lived. We keep mistaking namak for sugar, lal mirch for powdered color. I can spread all my toes across the ground. Everyone cooks at home. My dance instructor says that breathing makes our muscles feel better. He's new to this. Women have softer lips. Kissing them is soft feeling. Women are not safe in Delhi. There's nothing new about New Delhi. Women are not safe in Bangalore. Muslims are not safe. A seven-year-old boy was beaten to death in Kerala. Asifa Bano died. Jyoti Singh died. I'm at home every day. There are safe areas in Bhopal, Patna, Hyderabad, and Ferozepur. It doesn't matter what you wear. Day and night are concepts for fools, 12 pm is as bad as 12 am. 12 am is as good as 12 pm. I'm reading progressive books. My brother is not. Mango is the king of fruits. He visits us only in summers. 15th Road is called Gulmohar Lane. Our bodies are made up of 75% water even after crying relentlessly. There are crystals for healing. The government is the same everywhere. A dictionary is enough. A constitution is not. Parrots are green. We have something against green. We massage dead bodies before burning them. We feed goats before eating them. Flowers are immature fruits. Shillong doesn't have red-light areas. 1/4th tsp of haldi is all that's needed for any recipe. Cutting your hair short doesn't make you feel lighter. Smoking makes me feel like smoke. Dragonflies bring emotional and spiritual maturity. I want to call someone honey. Fire cleanses the aura. People have died after a gas leak. There is truth hidden in every lie. I ate the flowers that grew with coriander leaves.

First published in *Epiphany*, Feb 2021

AMIT SHANKAR SAHA
Dissent in Good Faith

Quarantined thoughts dissent: slowly
spreading into a distanced sky—

line of rolling clouds. Tomorrow
the ministry of the thunder—

birds will rise like a theorem
of thoughtlessness, being governed

by laws as ancient as the hill—
mines that dot the gangrene land.

Escaping incarceration
in camps between this land and sky,

a note of dissent amidst words
of a judgement, like the cut wings,

neither fall nor fly but hang on
the soft winds in good faith.

First published in *Witness: The Red River Book of Poetry of Dissent*, Edited by Nabina Das, 2021

AMLANJYOTI GOSWAMI
Bus Routes of Childhood

Machkhowa: Fish eater.
Dighalipukhuri: Long pond. Not Silpukhuri: Stone pond.
Or Joorpukhuri: Twinponds. Nak kata pukhuri: Chopped nose pond.
Ambari: Mango garden. Bharalumukh: Mouth of river.
Sharab Bhatti: Booze joint.
Adabari: Ginger garden. Near Jalukbari: Pepper garden.
Jorabat: Stitching ways. To the hills where the air turns cold.
Teeni aali: Three alleys. Saari aali: Four alleys.
Bijoynagar: Victory city. Swamped by the flood.
Barowari: Twelve come together (for a cause).
Pan Bazaar: Betel leaf bazaar. Books housed in childhood.
Aath gaon: Eight villages. Can't find any.
Puronigudam: Old godown. Near ma's place.
Palashbari: Garden of palash flowers. Dad's place.
Khatiamari: Where the deer was killed.
Santipur: Place of peace. Near a hospital, a football field.
Nagaon: Nine Villages. Where ma comes from.

Bus routes of childhood. No place to sit, standing room only.
        On the ledge, breeze on hair.
Travelling tomorrow with yesterday's eyes.
Crossing fairytales along the way, but never knowing.
        Not paying a penny.
The bus stops at odd, dusty places, looking for memories.
        No passenger in sight.

Come one come all, the conductor screams.
There are no mango gardens, victory cities, villages left.
        They were gone when I came.
Ways no longer knit on their own.
The old ponds remain, feelings dip, mirrors face the past.
        Carrying sirens at midnight.
Once upon a time, there was no city. There were only
        dreams, gardens, a flower market.
And you still ask me, why do I like it so much?

First published in *The Poetry Review*, April 2021

ANANNYA UBEROI
Gratitude

There is a ruddy fox outside my doorstep.
In her fox-fur, she yelps, her bleak, oval mouth
digging into the powdered snow. Shyly, she finds
a cricket ball and holds it up on her nose.

There is a squirrel's nest stuffed between my window grill
and the hard glass. The mother has gathered green twigs,
leaves, bark, and soft moss from even beneath the milk-tundra
to bed her babies when they are formed.

There is a snow bunting who comes for
spiders and flower-grass from my patio. I leave her
warm water on the bird bath, she flies low even when
I'm working the wood—there is no fear.

She leaves with a silent nod,
a bob of the head, a demonstration of gratitude to the ruddy fox
nestled in a duvet cover in a dogshed beside the bird bath,

now silent and slow, eyes narrowed in near-sleep,
mistaken, once again, for the lessor of a fair winterhouse
of flax and sunflower chip.

First published in *Columba Poetry*, Issue 6, Winter 2021

ANJALI PUROHIT
Warren

This morning I noticed there was a tunnel that runs from my
house to yours

my desires discarded every night as worthless as used
condoms on the brothel floor lay heaped against the wall in a
corner hiding the cavity so expertly like a magician who
shoots an arrow and it flies in the opposite direction seeking
vengeance from a day filled with monotony looking for
escape for it churns a hunger as turgid as the seeds in the earth
when girls become women and women become girls while the
river flows oblivious to the light that falls on its waves
wanting them to rise and birth a hundred sons yet the earth
births a daughter who will stay close to her side and share her
ache since the black soil is wet with humus and sweet is the
smell of decomposition that leaves a skeletal filigree behind
as delicate as she has been but eventually they are only bones
for the flesh has disappeared some torn away by hyenas who
must feed their passions and the rest given willingly in
bargain for pleasure duty or buying peace and respite from a
thirst that will never be quenched even by a thousand rivers a
thirst that rises from the depths of desperation and fear that
rises from deprivation and the dread that she will be cast out
with such a weak hand against an opponent who holds all the
trumps and yet

she lifts the mass in that dark forgotten corner where she
discovers a tunnel that she can pass through to reach your
home from mine and that each home has a tunnel we can join
up an endless catacomb a subterranean network if only we
uncovered that heap lying discarded in the dank dusty corners
we were so afraid to look at

First published in *Still we Sing*, Voices on Violence against Women, Feb 2021

ANKUR
The Long Sleep

She waits there shelling peas,
in green-grass sweetness, sinking-sun forgiveness,
while men with rifles march and mill round her.
The train that brings him home will never come;
she may well know it—silence descends bespoke—
yet she stays, a final evening of moving her hands for him.
Limpid stars have now broken the curfew as
her centuries-old hands peel the cardamom, break the nutmeg
the same way her great-grandmother did, a gauze of cotton flesh—
the house had roared then, booming voices, a wedding in preparation—
now the village was still and dead, a long winter had set in
and he wasn't here, the spring would never arrive.
There she sat, falling into a doze before the great sleep,
not even hearing the shot fired—was it a stray man, stray dog?—
and she quivered now and then, in cold and dreamt memories.
Soon they held her cold body captive, and
a koel sang—was the spring to come? now they trembled,
and they wondered about the unseen—
but then they looked around and felt reassured—
all quiet save for the innocuous floating cloud,
nothing but an old stove destined for the scrap.

First published in *Rattle*, Issue 73, Sept 2021

ANKUSH BANERJEE
Cyst
for S

Cyst— a word
we weld

with something like
hunger. Schist—

the texture of
Pangaea chapattis,

Shampooed lentils.
Mist— fate's

anaphora veiling
a fibroid-ridden uterus

slowly changing
everything. Kist—

where we hid
when we pained,

our supple hearts becoming
a site of learning

throbbing with knowledge. Kissed—
by a vacancy so large

we could smell it
on windowpanes. Palms,

psalms, paeans, prayers—
the gist— of a million

helplessnesses that
childhood of all ages

is heir to. Blessed—
when she took her first steps

saying, *now that I am better
let me cook for you.*

First published in *Usawa Literary Review*, Dec 2021

ANNA LYNN
Orphaned Fruit

Her stomach is a love letter to five children. They bulge by
the time of seven grandchildren. By the slight morning, she
drinks a coffee milk-less, bitter.

In the kitchen, she inspects the black balls set to dry (jackfruit
pulped, boiled, balled), bananas cut to wither into themselves,
prawn dried and powdered, left on yesterday's newspaper.

(You must choose the middle pages; they are the ones least
touched by hand)

The yellow meat is sweet, cooked in jaggery and coconut
shavings, two grandchildren walk into the kitchen to steal
them before they are dry, five don't like them.

Red meats are welcoming to the palate of all—sons, daughters
and in-laws. Flakes of chilly, hairs of ginger dissolve into
muddy depths of meat and fat. Sadly, they aren't polite to her
own stomach.

Since the husband's death, two summers ago, she oversees
coconuts sent to the mill. They will arrive later tomorrow,
along with the finely powdered rice, ten litters of virgin
coconut oil, five kilograms of powdered rice, five hundred
grams of rice, fried and dried and powdered. (no, they are not
the same)

Her eldest granddaughter is a picky eater. But she takes photographs for that thing they call Instagram (it is a kind of Facebook for photographs). The murdered cinnamon stem, stripped of scented bark; Pearl spot fish coated in blood red masala (ginger, garlic, salt, red chillies ground by stone); then wet flour, with impressions of bent fingers, held by Banana leaves.

The young one eats only the fried fish. Her own stomach does not prefer fins swimming against the currents of life.

Her children live in gardenless cities. She lives by the ghats over the seas that bring monsoons. Processing food, packaging litres and kilograms to be shipped into that cold, dry city of shoes and ties.

Her stomach, a globe of its own.

Unpeopled, warring for one more day of breath between spice and sugar.

First published on *The Chakkar*, Aug 2021

ANTARA MUKHERJEE
A Man's Cry

The day the men rolled cowries to save their kingdom
They pledged a woman as a luminous token

The day the white soldiers hulled their victory
The nautch girls bled between the sheets

The day little Nawab sprinkled some Old Spice
The hopscotching girl grew to tackle her neckline

The day the clerk was sent back home
His wife was handcuffed as a gelded goat, later made to please

Who says a man cannot cry, can't feel?
Scuttle for his emotions in a woman's sufferings.

First published in *The Chakkar*, April 2021

ARANYA
Searching…

google knows what I did last summer,
the fragrance of my soap. It knows that I'm hungry
even before I do. The state has ten national agencies
peeking into my computer (for my safety, of course).
Restaurants, banks, hotels, cinema halls, cafes
are in hot pursuit, a hiccup away. They're
discussing where I've been, where I'm going.

But nobody can tell me where Najeeb is.

First published in *Usawa Literary Journal*, Issue 6, Dec 2021

ARUN PARIA
Flawless

All my life, I wished to be flawless.
Like Schiller was flawless,
like Das was.
When father died
I hid in a room,
wrote a poem.
Mother wept
till dawn.
Then I slept.
After life's magic
act was over,
a man from the crematorium
came with a long van
to push
open the doors.
He found,
bare-bodied—
laid in the morning—
two men in two different
rooms. Dreamless,
but without a flaw.

First published in *nether Quarterly*, Vol 2, Issue 3, March 2021

ASHWANI KUMAR
There Is No Country for Writers

Lies emerging from deception
Or the hidden beast in things—
What strange, terrible experience is the Truth?
Low-priced religious pamphlets scream
The excessive glories of civilisations—
A superficial order of ranks and chasms of our languages.

Sometimes I crawl on four legs
Studying glossy reports of workers killed in factories.
Erroneous conclusions, and false morality have filled
My adulthood with inexplicable sexual fears.
Anonymous, ascetic libraries of memories are spiritual prisons
And I am not allowed to sin before god.

Lacking semantic rigour
Unique numeric identifiers of books self-destruct themselves.
Pessimistic moles on my face have inhibitory effects
On the muscular growth of hermit's writings.
This is not something I was hoping for—
The advancement of art and literature.

Polytheists, monotheists, and infidels tell me
There is no country for writers.
Writing has become
Fake, fragile, questionable—
The impossible crime of attractive metaphysicians

First published in *Scroll* 15 Sept 2021

ASWIN VIJAYAN
Khajuraho
Found poem derived from India: Travel Survival Kit, Lonely Planet, June 1987

Chandellas ruled for five centuries
and even one with a burst
of creative genius. The sheer beauty
and the size of the temples

so intriguing, and them so liberally
embellished with bands
of exceedingly fine and artistic stonework:
gods, goddesses, warriors,

musicians, animals—real and mythological.
Apsaras appear
on every temple, pouting and posing
like Playboy models.

Mithuna couples running through
a Kama Sutra
of positions and possibilities, some requiring
amazing athletic contortions

and some just good fun. The question remains
of why and how
these temples were built here
a thousand years ago—

here, where there is nothing
of beauty or interest,
no great population centres and only
dry, dusty heat—

and who, having chosen such
a strange site,
lent their labour to turn dreams
into stone.

First published in *Witness: The Red River Anthology of Poetry of Dissent,*
Edited by Nabina Das, Aug 2021

AVINAB DATTA-ARENG
Son of

The part of the mind that is
infallible has been unkind
in general to my friends.
I always see them digging
furiously under the shade
of a large tree.
Their parents are, of course, already dead.
And I almost say to myself
"How lucky" but my mind is drawn
To loose strips of plastic fluttering
on some high branch.
And I say to myself
"dead or alive you'll be unlucky."
There is no part of the mind that is
kind or infallible.
Dead friend, friendly dread,
dear sound of furious digging,
day has barely begun and I already
cannot drink anymore.

First published in *The Bombay Literary Magazine*, Issue 2, 2021

Babitha Marina Justin
Flamingo Dance

I
watched
the flamingos
       of your
          lake-
             island;
                you fed them
                shrimps, snails, you
                  read out tracts of free
                  dom
                     mixed with hate; they
                        danced in clusters.
                           Winter froze your
                             brows, snow-
                                capped peaks, twigs
                                   ploughed ravines on your
                                      skin. I miss the swagger of
                                         my youth who walked away
                          with
                          the
                          spr-
                          ing,
                          I
                          wa
                          nt
                          to

spindle time,
wind him back
to golden yarns of
years that traipsed past me—
foolish and ready for jig,
flinging a flamingo
blanket over me—

without grace,
kindness,
peace.

First published in *EgoPHobia*, June 20, 2021

BASUDHARA ROY
Light

The seat of desire is everywhere.
In this twelve-by-twelve room we share,
every article exudes warmth.
Books, biscuits, rose-tinted wallpaper,
alarm clock,
even the split green gram
sending in a rush its dense forest
of milk-white shoots upon that table
has swallowed love's sap.
I have known you now a few months
and am learning to find
in the majuscules of your face
the assurance of all my days.
It is new, this land dancing away
under my feet as if it cannot stop, this urge
to make my skin some wall
against which you may lean awhile
pleating the kerning of stars.
When you are away, I tidy your dresses;
sometimes put them on.
Match your muffins with my skirts,
feel upon my chest the heaviness
of your breasts. It's a rare intimacy,
this candid conversation of clothes and form.
During a difficult period, you bring me
warm milk with turmeric, a hot water bottle,

placing it in the niche of my abdomen
where it belongs. In the daunting bazaars
you bring me to, I urgently seek your hand.
You allow, make room for my damp fingers
within your steady, smoother ones.
Our silence brims with a conversation
I carry each moment in my head.
It is only your recesses I can ever wish
to inhabit. I want to tell you that
in this teeming, relentless city,

you alone are home.

First published in *Berfrois*, June 2021

BHARTI BANSAL
Jatinga Bird Mystery

Every year local and migratory birds fly to Jatinga only to commit
suicide.
They die as the fog descends down the mountains around the valley,
like a bride
And they rush towards the giggling light, get hit by long bamboo
trees and die."
You see, the first time I looked at you from a distance, I knew you
were going to be the death of me.
I, like those silly birds, flew towards the halo of your being and
crashed on your body
A deep chasm that echoed the last chirps of dying birds,
a sad goodbye
I knew it had to be this way, your name sounded like a symphony of
a toddler than a warning bell
Jatinga, a small valley in Assam
Us, a hole dug in the mid of this fabric of world
Together we made a perfect pair for anything that could kill
mercilessly
Those birds, migrating thousands of miles
Across seas and oceans
Leaving their nests like little soldiers
Only to die in a war that nobody started
Are their dead rotting carcasses, casualties of not looking enough in
the direction where the dark births out of the womb of the light
Or is it just another mystery that people forget soon enough, a friend

who bids you goodbye, gifts you harsh words you ponder over
throughout your life and think if he ever loved you at all?
If we die together, is that even death or a celebration of it?
If we know we have no time, will we slow down and look at the
skies above and the land below?
Will we ever know who loved us the most?
Does ground ever complain for mass graves or does it accept its
fate?
Are these birds forgetful like me, return back to the same valley/
you in the hope that maybe one day you will love as you had
promised to?
But who can blame you
Aren't you blamed enough already?
You have blood of innocent birds on your hand
You have unfulfilled dreams hanging like branches from your
bodice, my father's pride, and my mother's laughters, all perched
on your shoulders like pigeons that surrendered themselves to
land years ago.
Jatinga, a paradise
You, my final resting place
Hand me the gun with no bullets inside
And watch me die still
For there is something so powerful about apocalyptic sky in your
hooded eyes
When doom is about to fall
When we split like butchered sheep
When you laugh and I bow down before your feet
Take the knife and run it across my throat
For you had me flattered on the first day
When a shrink calculated my misplaced emotions as fifty percent
depression
And I had smiled
There is something about finality of the last moments
Those birds know the difference

I always knew the difference
Yet we never stopped
Because regrets are mishaps of love seeking forgiveness
And we don't forgive easily, do we?

You see there is a reason why crematoriums and rivers run side by side
We all tend to wash away our last sins
Those birds become the victims
And I turn into survivor instead
We have the same tattered wings
Same blooded corpses
A final call for help
And a dying wingless fall to tell our story
"We mattered
We mattered
We mattered"

First published in *Two Drops of Ink*, A Literary Blog, 23rd Oct. 2021

BHASWATI GHOSH
Native Dialect

Because she couldn't bring
with her the waters of Sugandha,
the river in her village,
my grandmother brought along
utterances that smelled of
its moist earth. Togo, aamago,
eda, oda, komu, khaamu,
the tongue's catalogue of
frank intimacy. The city
ordained her to adopt its
lexicon—polished words,
their sandpaper finish a
burden of survival, like living
on dry land.

When her little sister visited
and Grandma broke into their
Barisailya patois, I heard songs
of home in the words.
Of boat races and river markets.
Of a nest I'd dreamt of in past
lives, amid simulated nostalgia.

I watch YouTube videos
by young Barisal natives
to open my ears to rivers

of spoken waves. Togo, mogo,
kyada, zaamu, chaaul, aaij, kaayil.
The voices are young, fresh.
I strain to hear my grandmother in them.

First published in *HELD*, July 2021

DEBARSHI MITRA
the flick of a lighter

in the ocean blue
of half lit rooms

our shadows gather
to sharpen their blades.

First published in *The Shore*, Issue XI, Autumn 2021

DEBASIS TRIPATHY
Foreign Language

my tongue twists English
into a tight knot in the auditory cortex   & my fingers
curl   it into a nest of matted letters   my identity
my speech   hardly decipherable   my beliefs
smothered in suspicion & self-doubt   my adopted language
my writing   silent & cursive   curdling & cursing
& intoning cuss words like prayers   the incense stick
in the censer   the smoke spiraling into cryptic scripts
i think   i dream vernacular   & then translate
high-speed   frame by frame   word by word
grammar & spell checks   insertions & deletions
they mock   the progenitors   they correct
my concepts   my phrases   i decode   i interpret
a mutation in the sequence   style & structure   a recombination
traits that differ   from my progenitors   & i am who
is ostracized   who is not seen as one-of-our-own
i am mutant   an error caused in the interpretation
of a primeval vocabulary   the pig reared in a sanctuary
to generate organs & corpses   for a market
which buys   in a foreign land   i write
bad   i talk worse   i am caught in limbo
between my goals and my status quo   an apparition alive
attempting to land in heaven   with a mortal body & soul
caught in a nowhere world   in a word vacuum
my languages my identity   crossbred & crossed

First published in *Decomp Journal*, Fall 2021

DEVANSHI KHETARPAL
If you should have to ask

I want to lose something.
The stones take turns

inside my mother's
tired body. I am

the ugliest woman
in the waiting room.

Anything that comes
with instructions

ends up somewhere
dead inside me.

First published in *Poetry at Sangam*, Dec 2021

DIVYANSHI DASH
no trace

a beach-house under construction stands as lonely as me it looks

sad full of ugly junk & yet hollow like an empty can of coke like a bro-

-ken flute my hands draw on the sand my name in cursive transience can

fuck off i believe in catching ghosts and finding bottles with messages on the

shore lost and abandoned since two thousand two the year i was born the year every

thing changed trust me i don't believe in promises but if i ever find a message in a bottle

a cry in distress i will dye my hair blue i will do it in secret my mother hates it my mother will

hate it she will scream and i will scream back the buses will forget to pick me up the next

day i will be found stranded sleeping on the beach tongue all salty hair all rubbish please

pinch me if i dream again i will run for the waves and water can be my lover i can

dance like a swan float like a piece of wrapper fold myself
into the tiniest person

ever i will disappear into the water my body all swallowed
up dare anyone

to find me this will become a landfill and nobody will know
i was here

First published in *Stone of Madness Press*, Issue 13, Aug 1, 2021

DURGA PRASAD PANDA
Furniture of Bone

The creaking chair
has so absorbed
the frail, old man

reclining still on it
that he looks
like an apparition

trying desperately
to fill in a vacant space.
Head bent low,

his lean, drooping hands
merge into the armrests;
his skeletal frame

shrinks awkwardly
into a furniture of bones.
The chair turns

into a wooden version
of a man slumped
down on all his fours.

Like two shadows
embracing each other
at the twilight hours,

and the sagging skin
of darkness gently covering
the furniture of bones

like a warm piece of blanket.

First published in *Speak*, USA, Issue 6, Summer 2021

FEBY JOSEPH
Dad's Chicken Mappas

Midnight mass and an overzealous Christmas meal
    Were the two things that bonded us
        Even when we lived like native refugees
In cities that owned us —   Dad pawned a few years
    To Muscat
Then Mumbai   finally Dammam
        There's a forgotten chapter of a journey from Kottayam
To Mumbai in his gypsy lifeline.

I used to hate the smell of heated ghee when I was small — those
    Eastman—coloured days of *Doordarshan*
Were scented by curried beef and the Christmas special —
        Chicken *Mappas*
        With white fluffy *appam.*

I fry potatoes, carrots, cashews and sultanas in batches — the smell of ghee
    Shapes into an ellipse curving through the early 80's
        And 1992   The year we let a desert own us
For the subsequent couple of Christmases in the *Hijri.*
        There's a forgotten chapter of a burning City
In our gypsy lifeline.

I read and fill the pressure cooker with chunks of gleaming pink chicken
And purple half-moon onions;
    Unholy amounts of ginger, garlic and slit thin green chilies;

an impressionists' palette of cinnamon and cardamom
and cloves and powdered pepper
and bay leaf and curry leaves
and coconut milk
and water
(*and salt*)

All from my dad's scribbles,
in a diary that emigrated from Dammam to Mumbai...
Dammam   Mumbai
Location never mattered much to a gypsy diary —
The pages surprisingly never turned
Yellow
And 25th of December   always smelled like *Mappas.*
There is an unforgotten chapter of a weak heart
That bonded two cities, a decade in, living under an Arabian Sun.

Once again I fall in love with *ghee* —
(My *Baklava* and
Basbousa memories...)
And fry onions with coriander and pepper and *garam masala.*
Somewhere   My dad's voice
Tells me when to tilt the pressure cooker
And mix the almost cooked chicken and stock into the fried spices.
His notes tell me to add the fried veggies and nuts and finish
With half a cup of thick coconut milk.

As a side note
He had written.   "Serve with hot *appam*"
Since Dad never wrote how to make *that* down
I have to rely on my mother...

We leave for midnight mass.   In Mumbai *that* means 9:00 PM
There's an unfinished chapter of a portrait
And expectations and memories and mappas.

65

Notes:

Mappas — An aromatic stew of meat and vegetables
Appam — A South — Indian rice based pancake.
Doordarshan — Indian State owned Television channel
Hijri — Arabic Calendar
Baklava & Basbousa — Middle Eastern sweets

First published in *Foreign Literary Journal*, May 2021

GAYATRI LAKHIANI CHAWLA
Sindh

Sachal rests in the cobalt blueness of the walls of Daraza

the city he never left holds his shrine

in her folded hands

seeking the divine.

Sachal breathes in the sienna brown lotus stem fritters

sold door to door by the weary vendor,

wrapped in withered paper

time warped aftertaste,

"Drink from the chalice of love,

intoxicated in the ebb of separation".

He comes alive in the folktales of Mumal and Rano

sung by Amma sitting on a charpoy,

smoking ferociously from a brass hookah.

She's ninety-four now, quilting an Ajrak mattress

inherited from the ancestors of her ancestors

umbilically connected to the land and its people.

Sindh, the land of Sufi saints

brazen and stark

a contagion of faith

bellwether of nostalgia,

raise your hands to the Lord in the sky above

Oneness is contagious and resides here.

First published in *Architectural Poetry Competition Series*, 2020-2021

GAYATRI MAJUMDAR
Clock Hand

What if we are dead already
and someone forgot to switch
the light on? Turn the gas off, or adjust
the clock hand to the exact hour?

Things lay wasted — trees weighed down by the rain
on a metal and sombre dump-scape —
and blue lips whisper into Akhmatova's ear:
"Can you describe this?" What if?
At moon set, a stomping Spinosaurus
comes of age — it must be normal again.
We inch forward along pathways
of parting seas shifting the clock hand
backward — a simple Houdini trick!

The watchmaker now puzzled
scavenges his lost face,
rearranging stale memories of cocoon-spinning
dance morphing to fly across dreams
of sleep and rust-bitten ammo,
its red-spotted wings coming unpinned
on a collector's wall —
it could be free. What if?

What if we are all dead
and the car's broken headlights
show what lay ahead
and the page remains,
unturned?

First published in *Chipmunk*, Aug 2021

GEETHA RAVICHANDRAN
Granny Bone

The house was an almost ant hill.
The old woman seeking yogic powers
stayed on, hobbling around—
denouncing the world—
ulcerous wounds, slowly eating her body.
She sat on the creaking swing and sang in her lusty voice,
the ballad of the king, whose marriage was called off,
as the cook forgot to carry a fresh sprig of curry leaves.
She chased away robbers, yelling out to them, to come later
when she was gone, as everything would then be theirs.
The house where the children had frolicked
while the brides sulked, as mice ran through the rafters
where the dead calf lay buried under the turmeric plants
crumbled in response.
The cuckoo listened intently,
as her voice climbed
up the trunk of the tree
and soared unbound, forever free.

First published in *The Literary Nest*, June 2021

GOPAL LAHIRI
Remains

1.
Almost without noticing
you have arrived and everywhere the light glows,
let your memory drums in the night
let the twilight colours dry
let people come, touch your feet
tell them how the nature divides the country.

2.
Maybe we know each other better
I read lying down, the book on my chest,
it is the third lung
opening and closing in silence,
memories are all muddled up
and the image is entangled.

3.
My time is a sad one of collapses
empty coffee pots are on the table
words fold up like bamboo mat,
the stars crumble, the dawn opens like dry petals
green leaves are dotted with blood
silence is now both sign and prayer.

First published in *The Madrigal*, Vol II, Roots, Dublin, Ireland, May-June 2021

GOPI KOTTOOR
Come, sit by my side

Like you used to.
A longing, like a tree
Spreads in the middle of the river.
The wind is zephyr, deepening lyre, and your lips,
Are turning to love songs.
Like you used to.
What a way,
To set me on fire,
In the middle
Of all that water.

First published in *The Antonym*, Dec 2021

GOPIKA JADEJA
Untitled

"Is my love nothing for I've borne no children?"
I'm with you, Sappho, in that anarchist land.
—Agha Shahid Ali

Move into a rented house in a foreign land and imagine that
you are making a home.
Tie a toran on the door frame. If there is no garden, plant
a Jasud and a Champa in pots. Here, you can even find a
Mogra plant. In the Botanic Gardens you can see an Ashoka
tree along with Orchids. Two years ago there was news of
people flocking to see the bright orange flowers of an Ashoka
in bloom in Choa Chu Kang. Not the tall False Ashoka that
the British favoured in India, a real Ashoka. The kind they say
the Buddha was born underneath. There are many large trees
here. Far from buildings, far from me.
Move into a rented house in a foreign land and imagine that
you are making a home.

First published in *Cordite Poetry Review 99*, Singapore, edited by Joshua
Ip and Alvin Pang, 31 Oct 2020

HUZAIFA PANDIT
The Night is a Song

The night in your song is a jasmine that blooms
on the roads to the summer
which lie between us.
In the silence of this night, don't call out to me.
Where does the sparrow return after the last siege?
It flies past the blood of the last dusk
and unfurls the doors of prisons carved in the cheeks of our sky.
In the prisons, we will dig
apart the rubble of the long night when we lay awake,
the cold in our hands blooming into paisley,
just as it does in currencies hid by poets in old books.
Come if only a moment. What to tell you of the ache of separation.
Soon, the night promises,
there will be one more day to cast summer off
in the gardens of long dead that bloom on the shriveled Dal.
Look ahead of you, exile stretches its arms
over the outstretched obituaries.
The river of our winters turns at the bend
of your mirrors, where we watch, blinded,
the reflections of past summer-moons
glide in and out. Like moths in poems written under candles,
we hold death by night in palms bound shut by spools of barbed wire.

The night is a wound that opens on the lips of your song sung between
us.

74

In the song
another road opens to us to cross over to the daffodils
that suffered at our hands.
Come Dilbar, the flowers are abloom, come once
We raised our forgotten nights in the dark from which gushed out
dried streams of blood that are our cries.
We have cried over the scent of stones
that bear witness to our names in the sheets of forgotten snow.
There we will die, we promise over our tears of quivering mist,
and there our blood will plant apples.
In their bruises, we will burnish
our story and wait for the night to end our story.
We will put our faith in the sparrow
that flies away and await its return to fly on the feathers of a dream.
The night is a prayer that flowers in our fields,
and when the prayer ends,
we will return and rewrite what the rain wrote for us on the rocks.
At the gates of Harmukh I await, I will offer whatever pleases you.

First published in *Poetry at Sangam*, Dec. 2020

INDU PARVATHI
The Frogs of Malabar

The newspaper says fungoid frogs
in Malabar have become extinct,
from the picture doleful eyes of a frog
deepen, straw yellow shine
on brown slopes of its body.
Years ago in Malabar,
in my grandfather's nalukettu
fungoid frogs cruised red-oxide floors
in fleets of black and yellow taxies.
During languid afternoons, they ferried
us news from the courtyard latticed
with sunlight where aunts conspired
over heaps of cashew nuts and laughter
as we made brooms from coconut fronds
by the cowshed with our mother,
the frogs feasting on insects swarming
from the slurry pit, waiting to hop forth
at sunset to shadowy grounds beyond.
The day we were asked to leave,
I remember
how grandfather paced the veranda
how some frogs peeped from behind
the pillars as we came out,
my widowed mother and three of us —

all young and bewildered.
I remember
the joy of finding a few in the bedding
how they shimmered in the dark
in the house by the fish market.

First published in *Punch Magazine*, Feb 2021

ISHMEET KAUR CHAUDHRY
Happy Occasion of the Happy Marriage of Giani Harbans Singh with Harbans Kaur

A photograph of Harbans Singh and Harbans Kaur
A man neatly dressed in a light-colored suit
And a woman with a 3-inch ghoonghat clad in a salwar Kameez
Circumambulating around the holy book
as a Sikh-wedding ritual
tying a wed lock
to be happily married.

This isn't a common photograph of any wedding
but of a wedding that stores the history of a Gurudwara
where many lives were saved
when riots began
during partition of India and Pakistan
as they took shelter in this huge building
with iron rods embedded in the walls

The overleaf note written with a fountain pen
on the photograph reads:
"Photo taken by Sarup Singh on the happy occasion
of the happy marriage of
Giani Harbans Singh with Harbans Kaur
d/o Chaudhry Gurdit Singh in Singh Sabha Gurdwara
Kahuta on 23/4/'43"

Four year after partition
In the fateful year 1947 called santali
the couple migrated to India.
They stole every news of their village
watching the saree clad anchor on black and white T.V. sets
or talked to the pilgrims
who had just returned from a tour to the Gurdwaras left behind.

One day they read the newspapers with teary eyes
that their ancestral village was cleared off
and so was the Gurdwara brought down
for erection of the Nuclear plant
of the newly formed Government, the new nation
in the name of its security and prestige
in the place they now called Pakistan.

The power games continue
and the powerless common people too continue
trying to make sense of their lives, their lost homes,
remembering the moments of love and laughter
with their friends and family, scattered now
remembering them seeing the photographs with
overleaf notes written in fountainpens.

First published in *Muse India*, Issue 97, May-June 2021

JAGARI MUKHERJEE
My Father Steals a Jackfruit

The colour of hunger is flame-red.
The red you get from burning coals or wood
to start a fire.
You'd think cooking comes easy to village folks—
except, when you're too poor to buy coals or wood.
Your actions soon turn into hundred shades of grey.
You learn in school that it's nobler to starve than beg.
Except the fire within won't give an inch of relief
as it eats you all the way. What does it take?

What does it take for a child to steal a jackfruit
in the dead of the night?
It's easy to tiptoe to a neighbour's garden
while mother at home drinks the Ganges
in lieu of a meal. A stomach demands to be filled.
You curb your shame and break off God's forbidden fruit.
Then, to the market in the morning to sell it
for half a kilo of rice.
I'll tell the famous poet that the world ends in fire, not ice.

Yet, you survive another day. Eat well.

First published in *Transcendent Zero Press*, Oct 2021

JHILAM CHATTRAJ
Aloo Posto

Imagine a mustard afternoon.

The kitchen, barefoot
On summer's breath.

Newspapers mumbling
between Baba's thick fingers

and you, beneath the high-blue
Bengal sky, wait moist,

for gorom bhaat, biulir daal, aloo posto.

It's no gourmet trick in delight,
but a famished melody of ancient wives.

The slow hum of poppy seeds
grounded to a mellow warmth

by Kajer Mashi on the sheel noda.
She, dripping beads of clear water

on the wet stone, wafting fragrance
of love, sleep and war.

Cubed potatoes, sliced onions,
a tender sauna followed by posto's

drowsy descent into a pool of pallid dream.
Its wood-bark aroma — a stoic ring

of lonely British sentries,
amid the rich blooms of 'aphim' fields.

Their cruel resolve, rising
in the steely cry of the khunti,

scraping sheets of posto-skin
off the kodai. Ma serves it in a baati.

A glazed, green chilly punctures
the air, crisp with the nutty whiff

of onion seeds on posto's soft, swollen belly.
This is what you came home for —

a distilled escape from the tandoors, tarkas,
the measured spoons of corporate dining.

Posto is a farmer's find,
unheard by Apps and delivery boys.

A humble hunger healed by potatoes
without the familiar sprinkle

of jeera, dhaniya, haldi and laal mirch.

Notes:

Aloo Posto: It is a lightly-spiced, traditional Bengali recipe of potatoes in a paste of poppy seeds. 'Aloo' means potato and 'posto' means poppy seeds in Baangla. There are different ways of making 'Aloo Posto.' The poem describes the one that I am familiar with in my family.

Biulir daal: A thick soup/broth of boiled, 'biuli,' a lentil variety.

Gorom bhaat: 'Gorom' means hot and 'bhaat' means rice (in Baangla).

Kajer Mashi: A common way of addressing the female, household help in Bengal (in Baangla).

Sheel Noda: 'Sheel' is a flat stone mortar and 'Noda' is the stone pestle (in Baangla).

Aphim: Opium. An allusion to British trade monopoly on Bengal Opium.

Khunti: A steel spatula (in Baangla).

Kodai: A bowl-shaped frying pan with two handles used in Indian cooking; a type of wok; (in Baangla).

First published in "The Porridge Magazine", Nov 2020

JINENDRA JAIN
Those Days

You can take all the rusting gold I secreted away,
for those monsoons until childhood slipped away;

those petrichor smells, flooded lanes,
and paper-boats that floated away;

those long power-cuts, roof-top cots,
and sultry summer nights chatted away;

those last-row wooden-benches we fought for,
and the whispers when teachers looked away;

those childhood vows of togetherness, JJ,
and the smiling faces that have faded away.

First published in *Rattle*, Issue 73, Fall 2021

JONAKI RAY
The Day I Found Out About Your Accident

for AM

I was lying on the bed halved the same way,
by the same winter sun that had lain across us.

A common friend monotoned about the bus
that hit you and the minutes you lay bleeding.

I remembered that first time you went missing,
and later, my screaming, "Where were you?"

You had understood then the cobra strike of memory,
of mother dead that winter before I reached her.

I watch you today as you lie strapped,
your urine leaking out of the catheter.

When did we become so busy measuring
the hurt that we forgot the want behind it?

First published on *The Alipore Post*, Winter theme, Dec 2021

JYOTIRMOY SIL
Ashwatthama in a Bar

You emerge again when the messages in
my android synchronize with the lost memories.
The red liquid has started to play with my nerves.
Measuring the meanings with footnotes
Sense the hollowness in some symbiotic ways.
Like the vague reflection in an old mirror,
The crumbled glimpses assemble like an 'Autumnal Cannibalism'.
Savagely deformed.
Then Ashwatthama walks into this bar and sits heavily beside my arms.
The stain of pain that his forehead has restrained through the ages,
The poison of curse still runs through his veins.
His eyes radiate the archaic numbness
Endlessly waiting for the end.
Silence creates margin...

Yet I perceive your stain.

[Ashwatthama, in the *Mahabharata*, fought for the Kauravas in
Kurukshetra. Once he threw Brahmastra to the womb of Uttara who was
carrying the child of Abhimanyu, the deceased son of Arjuna. Sage Vyasa
compelled him to yield the 'gem' with which he was born in his forehead,
and Krishna cursed him to be a chiranjivi (immortal). Ashwatthama, after
the war, exiled himself, and was fated to roam for eternity with the wound
in his forehead.]

First published in *Muse India*, Issue 95, Jan-Feb 2021

K. SRILATA
Says Madhavi to her Friend

Madhavi's story features in book five of the Mahabharatha,
the Udyoga Parva. Sage Galava asks King Yayati for eight
hundred shyam karna horses - white horses with one black
ear. He wishes to offer them to his guru, Vishwamitra, as his
dakshina. Yayati does not have these rare horses in his stable.
Not wanting to send Galava away empty-handed, he offers
him his daughter Madhavi who has the gift of being a self-
renewing virgin.
'Offer her to four men who want to be the father of a king
and ask them for two hundred such horses in exchange,'
Yayati tells Galava. Galava proceeds to "offer" Madhavi
to a succession of three kings, each of whom father a son
by her. Each king gives Galava two hundred shyam karna
horses and so the sage obtains a total of six hundred horses.
As for Madhavi, she regains her virginity every single time.
Galava gifts Vishwamitra these six hundred horses as part
of his gurudakshina. In lieu of the remaining two hundred
horses, he offers him Madhavi. Vishwamitra too has a son by
Madhavi. When her father offers to get her married to a man
of her choice, Madhavi refuses, choosing instead the path of
an ascetic.

prayer beads—
I forget
to keep count

With Galava, it was only a question of numbers.
One way or the other,
it had to add up to

87

eight hundred moon-white horses
with one black ear,
gurudakshina for Vishwamitra.

And that was what he sought from my father.
You know the rest, sakhi—
I became Galava's way
for it all to add up,
my body the gift that was bartered,
and since none who came to our house
returned empty-handed—
my father— you know him - is a proud and generous
man—
I went along, did his bidding.

Three kings over three years to sleep with,
and, in the end, Vishwamitra himself,
a son each with each.
What more could I ask for?
It all added up nicely for Galava,
and they said— it wasn't so bad for me—
For one thing, I was doing my duty as a daughter,
earning my place in heaven,
and I had lost nothing in the process
for didn't I go right back to being a virgin ?
What cause, had I, to complain?

I don't know who else to tell this to, sakhi, but you.
Some nights I wake to the feel
of cockroaches crawling on my breasts.
I think it is my skin remembering those men.
And they say I am a virgin
with no cause for complaint.

First published in *Poetry at Sangam*, July 2021
Poem nominated by "*Poetry at Sangam*

KANDALA SINGH
Birdwatching

My mother says it was the peacock
that did it, the reason I said *papa*
before *mama*. In the memory she made
for me, you took me to the chhat
and taught me how to say 'mor.'

I don't remember the peacocks. I remember wanting
parrots.

She insists they were why I forgave
you her bruises: red turning blue,
then green, color of rose-ringed
parakeets. I remember

pointing a fruit
knife at you, blade sticky
with orange pulp. I remember

the forests we crossed
every Himalayan summer;
how you taught
me to listen for a river;
joining tops of blue
pine to bulbuls who flew
across, drawing threads

with our eyes to trace
their flight. I remember
the shrill in *mama*'s voice

the first time she called my name
for help. I remember
screaming STOP.

I remember learning
to pronounce or-ni-tho-lo-gist,
you explaining you weren't
one. I remember breathing

sessions in therapy, sifting
summer from winter, you
from *mama*'s husband,
my therapist saying I should
hold on to the good things you did.

First published in the Winter 2020 edition of *Rust and Moth*.
Republished in *The Hindustan Times* on 4th August 2021

Karan Kapoor
Endlessness

He is endless, says my father, looking inside his glass. Inside
the wine glass is a forest. Inside the forest are many vineyards
and monkeys. Inside the monkeys, a lake of melancholy. Inside
the lake of melancholy, many women are bathing. Inside the
women are many disappointing male lovers. Inside the lovers,
a language of hate. Inside that language, an algorithm for
addiction. Inside the algorithm resides my father. Inside my
father, a cage. Inside that cage, my father, trapped. Inside the
father inside the cage, another cage. I did not mean to talk
about him through a necklace of onions. But he likes onions.
Isn't it fascinating, he exclaims, the way they seem endless up
until they end and nothing remains.

First published in *Atticus Review*, Oct 27, 2021

KARTIKAY AGARWAL
Khair (خیر / खैर)

The Urdu word that means *good*
and is said to wish *your well-being*,
is also used as an act of letting go.

The letting-it-be when a thought
that is somewhere between your lips
and the tongue, would rather be unsaid.

On a good day I would tell you that it means
to choose the being-well of the conversation —
that relationship — over the being-right of you.

Somewhere, 'خیر' would be the name of my home
—a place for love and light, where opinions exist
as a mosaic floor, and not half-eaten sentences.

Khair, I must stop lying—my tongue usually finds
the word, the way my hand looks for a light switch
when the room goes dark—to erase hazy uncertainty.

First published in *Jaggery*, Issue 18, 5th October, Fall 2021

KASHIANA SINGH
Woman by the Door

I sit by the door today
talk to myself

my voice quivers
as it reaches into the valley
where I had hidden you

I savor your ache, nuzzle you
swallow the leftover skies, of
canyons that were a fortress

I remember, in search for you
you smell of unfinished bread
pudding, the one mama made

each morning, of caramelized
sugar
and
toasted
bread

I open the door and the silt
of the outside, storms inside
the tablecloth is drenched

A penance breaks dam, unease
arriving in tears, of all the years
you waited by windows, your

arms barricading them from
the storm that brewed inside
I descend into the wet walls

of your waiting cries, like an
explosion fluttering into our
butterfly wings.

metamorphosis, even a butterfly
practices formlessness before it
arrives glossy as a monarch.

First published in *The Silent World in her Vase*, Dec 2020

KAVITA EZEKIEL MENDONCA
Those Bombay Sundays
(Inspired by Robert Hayden's poem 'Those Winter Sundays.')

Those Bombay Sundays
My father woke up his usual 'early.'
'Seize the day,' he would say.
He gave the Carpe Diem call
on other days too.
Oh, that rising reluctance
on those Bombay Sundays,
Resisting his poetic exhortations.
The crows and pigeons followed the rhythm
of early rising, no matter the day of the week.
Did he want me to turn into a bird?

Then the Black and White TV arrived,
A loan from the National newspaper,
Brought the entire neighborhood with it,
Mostly children, and all those related to them.
Grandmothers needed a helping hand,
to climb the old creaking, wooden staircase
But come they must, to watch the Sunday Bollywood movie.

Father watched the six o' clock movie,
to write his TV column,
The children sat on the stone floor,
Like groundlings at a Shakespeare play,
My aunt sat on the large bed, watching intently

with a grandmother or two,
Begged the husband not to beat his wife,
'It's wrong,' she would say in Marathi.
Calling out the villain to repent of his evil deeds,
Smiling widely when the hero chased the heroine
around the tree, singing romantic songs.
Shifting her weight to the edge of the bed,
when the tension was palpable.
Father wanted to know why the female singers had such high voices.

He had a bemused look on his face
throughout, and with steady stoicism
watched all three hours of the movie,
Took notes on a lined note pad,
Smiled at the children from time to time.

During the intermission
the children stood up, dusted themselves,
Quickly sat down again to watch.

In true Shakespearean groundling style
they called out different 'endings'
to scenes, each according to their tastes.

Those Bombay Sundays
Of the Black and White TV,
When loneliness was unknown,
and no silent snow was falling.

I hear the voices of the children
"Thank you Uncle, thank you Uncle,
See you next Sunday."
Daddy loved the children,
kept a few handkerchiefs ready,
for the ones with the runny noses.

"Please come again", he responded to their thanks,
A true Indian-English phrase!
When I say it here, I see the surprise
on the faces of my visitors
and I have to explain, it means
they are welcome to visit
again.
We say it in India,
Even when exasperated
by some in the constant stream
Of visitors!

First published in *Usawa Literary Review*, Issue no. 5, June 2021

KINJAL SETHIA
Maa stitched

different costumes every annual day.
Sometimes Spock, once a fruit vendor
and then Santa Claus, even a futuristic
laser gun wielder. Moulded to my size.
The delicate running stitch smoothened,
thread tails neatly cut for my comfort.

Hunched over a Singer-clacketing,
humming her favourite ghazals.
Each frock, shirt, the hem
and the attached lace- forgiving and safe.
Rainbow rolls of thread soaked
with her devoted instinct.

Every dress costumed a lesson,
an impress of her values and convictions.
The day she dressed me as Santa,
she spoke of his seasonal profession.
The yoke was a promise of autonomy,
an ardent oath she pressed into each fabric.

A thread broke, a knot
has made waste of all the moth balls
and her songs.

First published in *nether Quarterly*, 3rd Issue, Vol 2, March 2021

KINSHUK GUPTA
Case History of Pain

You should be able to pinpoint it: abdomen, upper half,
left side, a hand's breadth from the last floating rib.

Compare it with ballpoint's prick or knife's stab—
we were taught in medical school. That winter when the sun

bleached, and roads jacketed in snow, I saw a grainy green
chameleon on a branch, his beaded eyes peeling away

excuses that kept me spooning Plath's tulips. Leaving me
hungry for whistling Malabar thrush. Hungry for donuts

dunked in sugar syrup—sweet at first, then tart on tongue.
Hungry for wind saturated with salt. Your bent knees were peaks, and

my body moored into your valley;
borrowed the orchestra of your breaths—
in and out, in and out,   long and loud gasp.

That winter I feared greasy, five-toed depression. Its coiled tail.
Its pale, flaking skin. That winter when I asked my father to

drive me to the therapist, he told me: Bear, Bear like a man.
That winter, dread spread in mom's eyes,
when I rode shotgun in the car.

Friends wishing—Go to God. Begging in scented temples,
my prayers hissing in ears like clumsy bells. That winter I fell upon

dreams, changing colours—gunmetal sky, burgundy bruises,
pea-soup fog. That winter the psychiatrist said: Your disease is fictional.

Depression is alive only in black and white. That winter I kept
searching for lithe silhouettes as reptile's eyes scanned my body.

That winter I wished for wicker coracle of sleep. Dreamt of eyes
hidden in whopping cyclones. Woke up to eyes beaded in jet-black sky,

craving sleep again. Like a prisoner pardoned for a crime
he didn't commit. That winter before the chameleon cracked

whip of tongue, I learnt that pain is only pain with a name;
searched for sounds in the language sheltered in my bones.

It is unholy to think that the war is over when guns
stop shooting. When he rolled back his tongue to swallow me,

I kept running and running and running
                                                from the pistol of his eyes.

First published in *Inklette*, Sept 2021

KIRAN BHAT
2015

I came back to Mysore
not to visit
as I did since I was a six-year old boy
visiting Blossoms with my Akka
playing video games with my cousins in Mangalore
but to learn my mother tongue
which I never knew how to speak well.

one day an uncle took me to the park.
I was eager to practice
I threw whatever words of the language I knew.
He went up to a friend of his
and asked him to listen to me
to see if he could understand me.

one day I went with my driver to the sugarcane shop
no one understood what I said
my grandmother was frustrated
she told me to stop embarrassing her.

I got so mad that day
the house shook with my yelling
afterwards I was so angry
I locked the door to my room
and refused to come out.

her hair grayed ever yet
just like my nails.

I struggled for my language.
I lost hair over my language.
I ate my ego for my language.
I don't think it was worth it,
but a part of me changed,
and I don't know why,
because no one was nice,
and no one wanted me to do what I did,
but ever since then,
I have to go to India,
each and every year,
like it is my real country,
not the USA.

I don't feel like a native.
I don't always feel comfortable.
I probably look a little bit like a foreigner.

somehow I am still chained to it
there's more to it than racial appearance
there's custom, language, family

it is to be nothing and to be everything
to be someone and no one
to have it always recorded on my tongue
this contradiction
I was born and raised in the USA.
India is my country.

First published in *be:longing magazine*, 8 Nov 2020

KIRITI SENGUPTA
Line of Control

Strays recognize the regulars.
Road-side tea stalls house a convey of canines.
They chump or chew as walk-ins stop by.
Owner of the kiosk discreetly suggests
the stuff the mutts cherish.

My stroll to the cha shop is routinely challenged.
Curs from the neighborhood march along.
Affray crams the air.

First published in *The Lake*, Sept 2021

KUHU JOSHI
The Valley of Headstones

I am Hindu. They'll likely burn me
and my ashes will float on a river

unless they are heavy enough to sink.

I still have balm for my feet and arms, separate,
and one for my lips.

When I was diagnosed, the doctor said
my spine would twist and curve
till I stopped growing.

When Nanaji broke his skull on the road
the doctor said he would breathe
till he didn't.

In Lauterbrunnen, I saw my name
on an empty headstone

in the valley where mountains
met each other. Steep mountains,
growing straight up the earth.

There were many headstones.
Fog was moving in, its shadow
on some of the headstones, while the others
were white and sunny.

My brother's hair was curling from the moisture.
We saw flowers—red and pink Swiss blooms.

My brother took a photo of me.

In the background, a family
sitting at the picnic table.

The boy eating a bar of cheese,
the girl making rings in the grass
with her pink skirt. The mother
tearing bread, the father
calling the girl back.

Nothing felt wrong—we all belonged.

My brother took out two pears from his knapsack, waiting
for the family to finish
so we could take their table.

Mum and Dad would have waited too.
It wouldn't be right to sit on the grass
beside the headstones.

My body did not want to be burnt.

But there were no other sounds,
only the quiet the people made

under the earth, the family
chewing cheese and bread,

and us, waiting.

First published in *Rattle*, Oct 2021

KUNJANA PARASHAR
**It Is Allergy Season and God Has Harrumphed
a Giant Cough Upon Us**

I keep telling my friends of my uselessness, of the wastage of my hands.
I've only ever cared for the bills of sunbirds sucking the coral flowers,
or the way bellflowers look like gilded temple-bells, or the racemes
of a laburnum competing with the red silk cotton blooms waving
over Panvel creek. If I am near the end of things, let me admit
that I love watching the weather reports on television, the clouds
and the moving sun over Mumbai. I will do anything for a light
thunderstorm as long as the fishermen have retreated from
the intertidal, their nets heaving with clacking oyster-shells.
It is sad that I will never know of the breeding patterns of
bombay ducks. I will never study the wind-currents and
differentiate with confidence between the westerlies.
I want to pray so much but these days I am faithless.
I have been able to do so little, so abysmally little.
I have come to realize the stoutness of my hands,
their small, wanton grasp, their inability to
clasp a final prayer, to hold the evening
still in the beak of my short fingers,
like the chest of a lone rain quail,
watching the clouds gather,
readying for birdsong.

First published in *Poetry Northwest*, 15 Dec 2020

KUSHAL PODDAR
Ice-holes

The pond will never freeze. The phenomenon
keeps the coffee drinking, photo comparing and
internet surfing crowd from the cities and metros hot.
Tim regrets never ice-fishing he has read
so much about. We even crack dirty jokes about ice-holes.
The pond will never freeze. We caught Golden Rainbow Trout
last autumn. Leaves surrounded our ankles. Water
was already cold. Sun rose clean with a hint of peat and fell
like a finish of a cheap and young spirit we can afford.
The pond will never freeze; Tim circles the body of ripples.
Gentle breeze. Sun snows onto the ground. Tim's shadow
wins over his flesh. There exists his house,
if he takes the homebound trail,
I if he cares to call and kill time, his father if he wants to go back
to the job at their family tea stall, but he stalls time and lets the snow
shroud him, and this is it. I have nothing more to tell you this time.

First published in *EKL*, Issue 2, Dec. 2020.
Nominated by *EKL Review*

LAKSHMI KANNAN
Small Beginnings

I won't blame you
if you give me just a casual look
and move on.

I'm a tiny water body
four feet by four feet.
Yet, I was named Talakaveri*.

They knew I was a riverhead.
I've a shrine called Brahma Kundigai
that matches my infancy.

People throng to offer flowers, coins and prayers.
Come, you'll find me
on the Brahmagiri hills in Coorg.

I'll then start on my long journey
to wash equally,
the Kannada and the Tamil land.

Now that I know who I am
nothing can stop me.
Nothing.

*Talakaveri: source of the river Kaveri

First published in *Teesta Review*, A Journal of Poetry. Vol. 4, No. 2,
November 2021

LINA KRISHNAN
Falling

In that enchanted summer, for a five year-old visiting her
mother's brother, Shillong meant pineapples in the garden,
dog biscuits in the hall cupboard, and a real dog, oddly named
Kitty, to hug and to hold and to take for walks. It meant
living in a resin-smelling wooden house, with roof beams one
could touch from tall Mama's shoulders. Unforgettable plums
where the juice ran amok, and plum-cheeked babies tucked
into the bazaar grannies' backs, staring bemused.

Most of all, Shillong was about tumbling. The vast golf club
green, an extended backyard from the house, was a friendly
space where my new friends and I spent our days rolling
down the mounds and grassy slopes. On breezy days, we felt
as though our feet were almost airborne.

Six years ago, I returned for a spell to stay with a friend in
Shillong. The little town I remembered had changed, the
houses grown tenfold, and the road before Ward's Lake had
bumper to bumper traffic. And the hill path to my uncle's old
home, which in those days was marked by all of six houses,
had about a hundred now. I could not find it.

But the golf course was unchanged, mostly. The same faded
green shutters. The rolling vista. The emptiness. The grassy
slopes held out friendly arms. Could I, should I?

Roll down, down, down.

Find the child who tumbled and toppled

And plummeted without a care, down there

Way down now, and how does one even begin?

Not so easy letting go, with unthinking, trustful surrender

When did fear grow wings?

First published in *RIC Journal*, Dec 31, 2021

MAAZ BIN BILAL
Urdu

The sounds begin from Arabic,
Aleph, the first, aa,
(title later of Borges's stories),

Bey, the second, a Turkish title,
by Pe, the third,
we have left the land of Bebsi, and Bizza,
having traversed through Persia,

with Fe we have brought, the fun or skill,
to differentiate the phal from the fruit,
to Hindostan, now India,
where they germinated,
took root,
gone are Persian aspirations,
Jeem and Jhe are two distinct sounds,
Jute is what you may be wrapped in, to your grave,
Jhoot's the lie that surrounds,
which causes living death.

Jogi from Sanskrit is Urdu,
One that may bless you,
Train, from English, Urdu too,
from which Raj hangs out,
pleads: love is *mohabbat, ishq, uns, dosti,*
main tumse pyar karta hun.

First published in *The Hindu*, Nov 7, 2021

MALACHI EDWIN VETHAMANI
Odour of Rain

The evening rain arrived unannounced,
only the sound of water droplets,
on scorched roof tiles.
Then, it fled.

The parched grass,
now more disgruntled,
its roots stirred
by the odour of water.

Again, the sound of thunder teases.
Still no rain.
The over-worked air-conditioner
drones on.

First published in *The Saltbush Review*, Issue 1, Oct 2021

MANI RAO
Kashi after Dante

1.
Bhuḥ

Don't ask who's cooking tonight

at Harischandra and Manikarnika
holy confidential kitchens of Kashi

Shroud tears, skin sears
Juicy fat's oblation

Did marrow fizz
Fire, laugh

In three hours and a half
this human log

collectable
in a dustpan

For the first time I think to
count your eyelashes

to pluck them
before they're singed

Of each I'll make a
boat unmoored

Where in the worlds
are you

As if I poured a sky
of wax on you

Everywhere you are not
your exact absence

2.
Bhuvaḥ

In Uttarkashi

where sun dives and
pirouettes

and fish roll their eyes
dodging

tangled light doodles
We cup our hands

and drink Ma Ganga
infused

with arias of swans and
undertones of glaciers

Sweetness rises
Air floats sinless

In Kashi where

shadows hover anxious
like dogs marking

corners of terraced ghats
as lovers drink mirrors

A curly soot rains
upon the free bereft

and pundits claim
ashes still warm

from midnight pyres
for altar coffers at dawn

Hey Vishwanath of Kashi
O' Mt. Alchemy

Here I am, weightless
Now take me home

3.
Suvaḥ

So long as mountains meditate
this river will be wet

So long as boatmen paddle
a lullaby for the dead

Before sun strikes
and water turns cold

We row to a spot
churning upstream

Hand your ashes over
to the current

Ash can't swim

Hangs on to algae on hulls
Falls into arms of corals

Scraped and bitten by fish
Shat along gorges and flats

Why else do river beaches shine
What is mica made of

F.N.: Every day, hundreds of ritual cremations occur at Kashi's Manikarnika and Harishchandra ghats (banks). The mortal remains, i.e., the ashes, are then scattered in the river. The city's presiding deity is Shiva, called "Vishwanath." Some say the ash from midnight cremations is offered at the temple in the morning. Our cosmos has seven worlds, regrouped into three—*bhuḥ* (earth), *bhuvaḥ* (an in-between realm), and *suvaḥ* (paradise, always a beach) (can't say which, it's private).

First published in *Divining Dante anthology*, Recent Works Press, 2021

MANIK SHARMA
Grandpa and Grandma Sit on the Veranda

Grandpa poached a rabbit once, before turning
vegan; that picture is still on the wall,

alongside the photo which confirms
he got Grandma as well.

Pictures don't speak in names, but memory
becomes an old man's commotion.

Grandma probably declined to having any of
her photos put up on the wall

or nobody asked her, I didn't.
I just wanted Grandpa and Grandma to sit

on the veranda, where loftiness of slow lives
could, perhaps, be discovered. Grandma's chemise

had leafy sketches, of crack-opened skies—
Grandpa, probably, struggled to tell the difference

and looked up, occasionally, as if to confirm
the cracks were not in his eyes.

If not for the rain, or the bread they had
for years broken together, they refused

to step back inside. It probably scared
them both, that their coffin-fitting clothes

seemed wrapped, rather than worn. It scared
Grandpa to think, how easy it would be, to not

miss her when she would be gone. It scared
him more than it would be easier for her.

They were angry at each other for getting old, and
for having crumpled skin that read like trashed paper.

Grandpa, though, still liked to tell us stories of how
he had grown through dark years, and that Grandma

at that time, was the woman closest
to the sun-her rabbits, wet, in his shade.

First published in *Collegiality and Other Ballads* (Hawakal), Ed. Shamayita
Sen, May 2021

MANISHA SHARMA
I Had a Boy

Into layers of my makeup, I whisper

a girl is Shiva drinking ocean poison
and yet surviving as *neelkanth*, blue-throated

so, I had your brother
and dissolved you with a pill
dark blue running down the inside of my thighs.

First published in *Literary Mama*, March-April 2021

Meenakshi Mohan
Chat Masala
On Hyphenated Identity

Hyphenated identity with its complexities and simplicity is as old as human history; for some, the story is written in more linear scripts. For some, life moves in more inebriated curves. I dedicate this poem to my grandson Anant and many other kids like him. The fabric of modern society is slowly evolving – hybridity, which is compatible with hyphenated identity, is taking a turn in enriching rather than weakening the country. We may sing in the same tune as Maya Angelou's, "I rise… into a daybreak that's wondrously clear ….," and we can dream with Walt Whitman, "I hear America singing the varied carols. I hear …. Each singing what belongs to him or her … strong melodious songs."

My grandmother affectionately calls me her Chat Masala …
Why, I ask,
She tenderly expounds,
You are as eclectic as all my chat masala recipes!

Chat masala—
her favorite of all spices—
a mixture of various flavors.
A pinch in here and a nip in there
goes in all the delicacies her kitchen produces.
Italian, French, Mexican, Greek, Japanese, Chinese, Indian,

or name any—
I relish the chromatic results
this unique spice brings in her cooking.

How am I your chat masala?
Through her luminous smile, she illuminates
the story of my being.

Born in Singapore, childhood in Indonesia, India, England
Now, home in America—
a land of mixed ethnicity, race, culture, language, and religion.
In this deep-sea, of the variegated expanse
I am not anyone's "bird of a feather."
My DNA weaved with mixed color and texture—
not a melting pot,
but my own unique identity.

I speak in many tongues.
As a child, the first full sentence I babbled—
Akumav nasi goreng.
At four, I mesmerized my audience,
reciting Sanskrit Shlokas in a tongue of pure silver.
I often correct my father's Americanized Hindi.
I trick my mother with her Cockney heritage.
Spanish and French come with liminal drifts.

In the world of music,
I float from Bollywood to Hollywood,
from rock, nu-metal, 90's rap, soft pop to
Indian Blues and Remixes

Anthony Bourdain's adventure with universal cuisine fascinates me.
My palatability extends beyond
fish and chips, hamburgers, pizza, parmigiana,

NY strips, enchiladas, tacos,
moussaka to murgha Mussallem, and sag paneer.
Mexican, Italian, French, Japanese, and many more I love.

I am Chat Masala,
I love my grandmother's analogy—
So precise and pure.
I am a pinch of this and nip of that.
An eclectic mix!

I Am a Child of the Universe.

Note: Chat Masala is a spice and a mix of different ingredients used in Indian cooking, but now getting universal galore.

Akumav nasi goring— Indonesian. I want fried rice.

First published in *SETU*, Sept 2020 and republished by *International Writers Journal*, Year 2, No. 2, April-June 2021

MICHELLE D'COSTA
Somniloquy

I was a poor unfortunate soul until I met him.

Konkani slipped into my English like fat roaches
slipped under our door right after pest control.
When we dated, he told me I had to wipe out
Konkani from my system if I wanted to fit in
with his family. I poured home-made wine
from Mangalore into my mouth and emptied
my system of every Konkani word into the bottle's mouth.

Sealed it and abandoned it at the beach.

My voice is in a bottle the way Ariel's was in a shell.
My husband tells me, You need to see a therapist.
You've been talking in your sleep.
Did someone find the bottle? Do I name my exes?
You speak in Konkani. It disturbs me. It feels like
you're conspiring against me. I refrain from shutting
my eyes. I silently count bottles filled with Konkani

while he snores away in English, his tentacles, resting.

First published in *Berfrois*, Jan 2021

MINAL SAROSH
Haiku poem

cowbells...
one thought bumping
into another

First published in *Trailblazer Contest*, 2021

MOUMITA ALAM
Triangle

The tin roof of my never built
house is a triangle.
Its apex is in Chittur.
Every night being exhausted
when I type its door
an arm opens from the river near Palakkad.
I lie with my heart stretched
my shadow glimmers on Chittur Puzha.
Two arms dip into life or water
to give back warmth, colour and
smell of a house.

Two throbbing hearts at two ends
of a parallel line
and a giant tree above
we laugh, smile and cry.

Dawns break in
we return to our houses
we begin to shiver in the cold.

First published in *Love in the Time of a Pandemic*, *The Bibliophile Café*, June 13, 2021

MRINALINI HARCHANDRAI
Verandahs

Verandahs ought to be declared
the new world order
even though the old houses
birthed them as articles
of constitution wood

not in or outside
like thoughts can be
colonials of the brain
planting slap-paint rails
one can leap across

defender of the arts
of tea slurping
over fanning debates
weather the greenhouse
is a curdled film
of affected moss

table thudding parliament
of birding vocabulary
queuing intervention notes
of the robbin' tenderer
warbling black exchanges
from redcrest digital feeders

planters chair senate
spacing equitable expression
in a conclave of civil craft
empiring a democracy
of lounging lizards
in their folded arms.

First published in *Joao Roque Literary Journal*, 15th Feb. 2021

MUSTANSIR DALVI
Sunset Over Luxor

7.
Karnak steals light the longest, and then darkens, reluctantly.

6.
Temperatures invert Hatshepsut's platforms.
Hathor exudes maternal warmth.

5.
On the West Bank, every disturbed grave laments discovery.

4.
Ra's shimmering disc, like unhurried eons, fades over the Nile.

3.
Captains of feluccas lower sails, allow fire and water to bring them home.

2.
Tawrek and Sobek slip into the shallows without a ripple.

1.
The river reclaims its predestined role as a mirror of history.

First published in *The Silk Road Anthology: Ancient Egyptians, Modern Poems*, 2020

NABANITA SENGUPTA
Archived

We are
reminiscent yesterdays
upon an embroidered chiffon
that sits coy in a wardrobe corner

A heady smell from past
like an oversized overcoat
wraps the conversations
In the warmth of a wintry tea

through words freshly packed
we dish out old staples
That belonged once to
to the zone of reality

Yet now, in exile
Separated by time,
we speak a language
of *déjà vu*
and count the growing age
of memories, waiting
till the gates open once more

First published in *SETU*, Jan 2021

NABINA DAS
Even Bricks Need Love

1
After fog, heap, bridge, debris and rip
it seems love poems didn't need
that absinthe any more—
as much these sudden roads needed our sap
once through the isolation, their sleep.
Our love covered πr^2, nothing greater would suffice.
Come through that crack in the radius, you spoke—
across the blueprint of the fences, barricades
in the torn alley where civilisation is distilled.
Raise the cup, even bricks need love—
my hands blessedly drunk, our lips just on lips.

2
The belly of the earth is split open
behind my pristine (or so I think) terrace,
men at work, men howling, men
coming out of their shells of starvation.
That ancient act of food gathering—
but they still huddle hungry inside a shanty tarp.
A woman in an orange sari fills a broken bucket
only one man shouts, his spotless shirt, tongue whiplash.

3
When I say 'pain', he has already turned to the middle
page of The Second Sex by Simone de Beauvoir.

The siren has gone off for the ants to file out of
their human silos of grind— grain-less, stressed.
When I say 'soledad' means the sky cannot hold alone,
he reads aloud how in Haiti people are left to rot;
we're Blake's tigers, burning bright, only in desolation...
tearing our own sinews, snarling at the motorcades
in the forest of the night, we, our hearts gone concrete.

4
Take my bones, take and cook them
thick. Feed the broth to hunger's mouth.
Take the pores and seal them with hope.
Take the tarred roads grass-lined by my hair
dye them in your chemicals, faraway smoke stacks
factories running on flagrancy and fear, take
all my fingers and erect the traffic lights anew.
Make my eyes your morning once, then evening—
gem stones we will want to eat in vain. Take
this body of the woman who left, to come back.
To Hathras, to Hathras, bellowed the guy at the bus—
I was given a god to love. And that shibboleth fell
to the lilt of my heart-flower, wild wild grass—
take my tongue that burns: what's death to us?

5
Ask yourself— have you been breathing through
Your mouth or your nose? Also, see the smell of rain.
Ask yourself— what unknown hands will help by
Your side when you switch beds, the linen stark white
Bland like the ceiling above, while the IV pipe shakes.
Ask yourself— did the ambulance cries erupt high and low
In your dreams. Slow tears of those almost-gone, in pain.
Ask yourself— will you still taste, long for the same way
Your overpasses, pillars, walls, slowly crumbling in their seams.

6.
One whole year of lovelessness
One dream I had last night is of you
A curtain flying in the wind, it's a sea side
I taste salt from your roots and you too slake
Your thirst with the aroma I shed from my crevices
We talk food we didn't eat and love over heat
From our mouths. Outside, the city still waits like a hunter's trap.

First published in *Café Dissensus*, Dec 2021

NAMRATHA VARDHARAJAN
Srirangam

the
Gopuram
crowns the horizon,
his bosom unfolds epics
through sculptures in diverse hues—
He is the eye of your beloved, The banyan tree
among the grass, a High-rise among a sprinkling of dollhouses.

the
Cauvery
drapes this
ancient abode like
the nine—yard saree
worn by her sun—adorned women.

drafts of
dust, cow, hay
incense, camphor, sweat,
melting ghee on hot *akkaravadasal—*
waft into you as memories. Amber music
scents the air, reverberates your soul. The noon sun
scalds feet that scuttle across the paved paths. A coolness,
a serenity descends upon you in the hall of a thousand pillars.

Four
roads
lead to and from
the entryways of this
sandstone fortress of peace.
Maroon patios with stout pillars and
terracotta tiles crouch close to each other,
their paints chipping off at their seams. You wonder which of these windows
were broken by the cricket balls, batted on them by your forefathers.

A
hundred
thatched, low roofed shops
with wares ranging from iron cookware
to plastic toys, line the stone pathways on either side.
You sit at a bangle stall laden with more hues than a Crayola box,
trying out purple glass bangles with flecks of gold, as a man stoops under
the tube light and with a friendly smile of paan—
stained broken teeth, urges you to try "one more" dozen.

the
tourist,
(me) has an
(inexplicable) moment of belonging,
of coming home, in this birthplace of my
grandfather. I have eaten his melodious tales
with relish and glee, and digested it. Here are roots that could water me.

the
plunder
and the rise,
the looting and the reconstruction
of this sanctuary, over and over, the water tanks
that sustain themselves and the fish that help clean up—
are teachers for this broken soul that wandered through dark alleys in search of nothing,
Even scriptures carved on stones are worn away by the waters(of time),
I thirstily gulp down the essence of this land of grand old fables,
even as my grandfather and his stories
slipfade
away.

Gopuram— In South Indian architecture, the entrance gateway to a temple enclosure.
Cauvery— A river in South India, rising in the Western Ghats and flowing southeast into the Bay of Bengal
akkaravadasal— A traditional sweet dish prepared by cooking rice and lentils with milk, ghee, sugar and jaggery
paan— is a preparation combining betel leaf with areca nut widely consumed throughout South Asia

First published in *Around the World: Landscapes & Cityscapes*: 200 Poems from Poets Around the World Paperback by Steve Carr/Sweetycat Press, October 28, 2021

NANDINI SAHU
Ahalya's Waiting

"Ahalya, you will live here for many thousands of years,
eating wind, without any food, lying on ashes
and generating inner heat. Invisible to all creatures,
you will live in this hermitage. And when Ram,
who is unassailable, comes to this terrible forest,
then you will be purified. By receiving him as a guest
you will become free of greed and delusion,
you evil woman, and you will take on your own form
in my presence, full of joy."
Echoed husband Rishi Goutama's command
bestowed upon the beautiful wife Ahalya, who had just had
her first ever orgasm, the fulfilment of her
womanhood through Indra, in disguise of Goutama.
'Ahalya', the 'one with no ugliness'—
the woman beautiful turned into a stone there and then.
Reek of patriarchy with
the social game of victim-blaming began.

I am Ahalya. Am I really waiting since centuries
for my salvation by just a touch , and thus my redemption?
I have the Indriyas, the five senses, inside me
so solid that I cannot be transformed to oblivion,
I am as inert as a stone.
While my acquisitive mind retorts, my steady mind waits.
I am the Sthit-pragya Sadhak, I have my Indriyas
in my own accumulation.

Doing my sadhana, I am time and timeworn.

Oh Ram, finally you are generously plentiful
to meet me, after ages of waiting. But my penance
is not yet completed. I will not consent
oh Ram, to be redeemed by you for an offense
that I have not committed.
I am untainted, confident and clean.
What purity on me will you assign?
What is the merit of this debate on of my pollution?

Oh Ram, the archetypal Ram,
if you really need to touch me,
touch me as the elemental woman. Touch me
as the galaxies do collide, touch me with
all your unspent unbiased emotion.
Touch me as the blue firmament touches the stars.
Make me your lyre and lure me.
Give my harmony your personal touch.
I assure you, you'll solve the mysteries
of the universe with my touch,
because I am the quintessential, ultimate woman.

Your touch should be your creative language,
your behaviour, your basic attitude.
With my touch, stars ought to dance across your skin.
Your touch must take away my fears of
all Goutamas and Indras.
Love, soothe my anxiety and
fill my senses with your compassion.
Touch my cognizance and you can redeem the stone.
Make me your Muse.
You know, touch is where miracles arise
And exchange of the light and dark begin.
The curse of Rishi Goutama may be immobilized
with your touch, with this assertion.

My redemption lies not just in your touch
but in zero tolerance of
any marginalization.
I need a rejoinder from the society
and from you, oh the most knowledgeable one,
for my quintuple patriarchal relegation.
Father presented me, the puppet, to husband on his free will.
Husband couldn't fulfil me as a woman.
Indra tricked me to satiate his desire, not mine.
Inept, impotent husband cursed me
with what right, oh, with what right,
to become a stone exactly at a moment
when I was satiated as a woman!
And now why do I need yet another man, you, oh Ram,
to touch me and cleanse me of my uncommitted sin?

Touch sensitive, touch deprived,
touch-waiting, I would rather wait till eternity.
I prefer to reject your offer of touching me
on the condition of taking me
into the snares of purity-pollution.
I am my own possessor, proprietor, I am my woman.
Let me remain ethically upright on my own terms—
this is my ultimate liberation.

Reference to Goutama's curse:
Splitting the Difference: Gender and Myth in Ancient Greece and India
— Wendy Doniger, Mircea Eliade Distinguished Service Professor of the
History of Religions Wendy Doniger, Wendy Doniger O'Flaherty —
Google Books

First published in *SELECTED POEMS OF NANDINI SAHU*, Signorina
Publications, April 2021

Neeti Singh
City Script, an Excerpt

Eagle wet-winged, swoops in
through the curtain of arterial dream.

The continuous fall of liquid,
splintered sliced moons
spread-eagled on Hyundai panes.

The incoming breath and burden
of needs, what will happen next?

Who will buy me parmesan cheese
and feed my appetite for Rilke's
poems, orchids, red wine, raw silk?

The sinuous spin of yarn and sin,
paper-laws of gender justice,
the trail of Raga Darbari down the street,

the drum of rain on tin roofs,
and plastic—an army of rising stench—
rag, garbage, gareeb.

A sneaking pair of love birds kissing
behind a neem tree,
rain and dusk and an open urinal.

Make me a cup of sweet tea—
adrakcheenichai in a sublime overboil.

Tea takes its place as national heritage,
with forest lions and peacocks
rummaging in the shrubs for snakes.

First published in *Tiger Moth Review*, Singapore, Issue 5, 2021

NEHA R. KRISHNA
the skin

the skin of my poetry
bears the account of all scars
of my ex lovers' teeth and nails.

you are here today to seek
a triumph over this.

tracing the dates
squeezing the suns
learning the scars
trimming the nights
the wolves pause under your nails
with mouthful of blood
dripping flesh.

gliding over the ruins
exploring the earthiness
contouring the map
shelling the scent
the snail retracts back in your mouth
after moisturizing the edges
of the scars.

the grammar of your breaths
whitens the canvas of my sighs
and you,
you paint forest

on the skin.

First published in the anthology, *The Shape of a Poem*, Red River, Edited
by Srividya Sivakumar and Paresh Tiwari, June 2021

NIKITA PARIK
Chimera

(For the hours spent with Tannistha in the premises of Makkah Masjid, Hyderabad, Telangana)

Between *Maghrib* and *Isha* that day,
we may have sailed through
the ambiguity of linguistic living.

My consciousness— no, not my *rooh*,
but my *khudi*— may have taken flight
at the Muezzin's call. It may

or may not have flitted out
of my brown pupils, past
the borders of our bodies,

past the granite solidity around,
past *chai*-sellers, dream-vendors,
and high minarets in ochre and gold.

It may or may not have overseen
our covered-heads leaning
into each other, the pink of my *dupatta*

touching the blue of yours, before
swooping back to the ground
to where we were. Between

Maghrib and *Isha* that evening,
we may or may not have
lived an illusion.

First published in *Ekphrastic Review*, 1ˢᵗ June 2021

Nishi Pulugurtha
TIME

that thing that moves right up above my head

moves slowly

there is a noise as it moves

through the broken window I see green

leaves. they move, they shake

brightness comes into the room

looking at that window I try to get up

slowly. a voice comes to call me

she looks at me and asks why am I lying down

it is time to bathe

no it is not. it is time to sleep

look at the time

where do I find time

look at the clock. where is the clock

what is a clock

there on the wall. see it is there

it is time for a bath. I linger on

she keeps calling. Come, Come

her hand is held out. she does not listen

she takes me with her

from one room to another into another

into a small one

she makes it bright and takes off my clothes

she talks to me about my village, about ma

and then she pours water

that I don't like. I hate it

why does she do that

I want to sleep now

she goes on talking to me

but I am angry, I don't want to bath.

let me alone. she goes on— we need to have a bath

I will, not now. now is sleep time

why doesn't she listen

no one listens to me

I push her— I don't want here

I want to sleep

no one listens to me.

Published in *Witness: The Red River Book of Poetry of Dissent,* Edited by Nabina Das, 2021

PERVIN SAKET
Why Eating an Apple is Like Eating the World

With the first bite, as you break through skin and red,
you know what it is like
to consume borders.

At the second bite, when the juice flows down your chin,
you discover how rivers
contour the fall and fall of flesh.

Third, and you feel the hunger of those
whose apples are shriveled
or rotten. Vanished.

Next, you inhale the whiff of farmhands
you've never seen, as you ride
the alkaline loneliness of the seas.

(Perhaps that is why)
by the fifth bite, your mother
is not someone you're trying so hard
not to become.

The sixth bite and you're determined
your children will inherit a world
with apples in it.

With the last bite, as you count the seeds
scattered in your palm, you realize
no one can count
all the apples
pulsing
in each seed.

First published in *Tiferet Journal*, Autumn-Winter issue, 2020

PREETI PARIKH
The Migrant's Origin Song

I come from cantonments, jongas and jeeps, one-ton and
three-ton trucks hauling military engineering equipment—
I come from bridge construction sites, the mile-wide
Brahmaputra river flooding, army helicopters summoned
for rescue operations— I come from the words *forces* and
civilians— I come from small hill stations and capital
cities architectured by British colonials— I come from
joint families and ancestral homes long razed and replaced
by millennial buildings— I come from misri, panjiri,
nutty wheat flour roasted on iron skillets— I come from
pine trees, morning bugle calls, blanket and bedding in
hold-alls, trunks, hole-in ground toilets— I come from
8x10 hostel rooms, immersion rods warming bathwater in
buckets, laundry drying on clotheslines, benches on stepped
terraces— I come from power outages, inverters, petromax
lamps— I come from backyards with jackfruit trees, rows
of bathua, carrot, cauliflower, pepper plantings— I come
from home kitchens with makeshift temples and neem leaves
steeping in saucepans— I come from the northern plains of
the Ganga, from the waters of Teesta, Chenab, Tawi, Jhelum,
Yamuna, Sabarmati— I come from desert sands billowing
into turbaned heads and veiled eyes— I come from sleeper
cars in narrow gauge trains, water in matkis, and chai in
kulhads on platforms— I come from childhood collections
of coins and erasers, first-day postal covers, books amassed

and circulated amongst school friends, a precise one-to-one bartering— I come from the family motto: *Help others, and God will take good care of your life*— I come from questioning God, questioning life— I come from curfews, communal riots, immolations— I come from an undivided Indian subcontinent— I come from partition; I come from separation.

First published in *Ruminate Happenings*, March 2021

PREETI VANGANI
Unrewarding

From my father's cupboard,
I fish out the familiar purple tin,
heavy with his old coin collection.
Let his vintage piggy-bank waterfall
into a pyramid of silver on the bed.
Aanas, athanas, chavanis from when
a gallon of milk was a chavani. Sparkling
gold ginnis. My favorite though
is a one aana coin that he, still in school,
threw on the tracks to see what a fast train
would do to the penny. It is important I think,
for me to like this blanked metal, a little
crimped moon. Because it reminds me
that my father, the constant harbourer of hurry
and worry, the man who plots to leave
a room as soon as he enters it — once stood still
as a summer afternoon — back of his knees
sweating sweet, tapping his feet at the edge
of a railway platform to simply observe
the workings of pressure. Just as he sat,
rocking his chair, slow as a lullaby,
for three months and change by mother,
comatose in a non-AC hospital room.
By then he was done running
her memory back by purring the songs

she loved. By then, the only song
was him waiting and his resting
heart like an empty bucket poised
to be filled with the water of courage.
What is his exit strategy now? Where does
he hide his sorrow? Between the same
molars that once thickened as honeycombs
with mum's roti crumbles, deep fried
in sugar and ghee? Kutti — we call this
rich breakfast. And dad's salesman-superstition
is to absolutely eat *kutti* on the first
of every month. Kutti on the tongue,
he used to sing, means Lakshmi will come
chhanchhanchhan. Once, he sang
for more money. Once, he sang for more
of mummy. Now, before work, he gulps down
three Marie biscuits, a glass of milk. Rubs his belly
says, I am superbly full. He knows he isn't.
He knows I know he isn't. Fullness,
his currency of consolation, his way of saying,
I know we're grieving for your mother,
but I don't want you to
also grieve for my hunger.

First published in *Portland Review*, Issue 87, March 2021

PRIYA SARUKKAI CHABRIA
Song 58

Let all joy mingle

Joy
that makes earth flow
in grass

sets life and death
dancing

that throws
everything it has on the dust

that knows not a word

~

in

my last

song

                                    joy

                        sits still

                on the open

        red lotus

of pain

First published in *Sing of Life Revisioning Tagore's Gitanjali,* 2021

PURABI BHATTACHARYA
Then I was not the antagonist in your fiction

Pine needles. The hill breeze. Take me home. It is winter
and this has been a while. This silly disorder- nostalgia

On a plateau purple peppered, mountain harebell stare;
I remember brushing with my finger on a canvas as catholic as the sky
a dreamland underneath the blue, punctuated by flocks of cloud.
I dreamt. No. I lay on my land,
much before you called me an "outsider"

I have missed winters for long, long time. You
stole my pine song of December and placed it
on the entrance of the neighbouring cemetery.

The snow on stripped jacaranda tree looks odd.
Choler clutches a branch.
You too run for cover and find a way to my inked patch.
Unfenced. Unmanned.

Remember the times we shared full clad peach trees.
We shared its sweetness. Its green.
Then you didn't find me a child of the ill-fated refugee.
Then I was not the antagonist
in your fiction.
We could sit down quietly. Cheek to cheek.
Free our feet. Dunk into the watershed

our secret spot.
You and I shared words. You and I shared dreams.
Wrote poems on love
stealing adjectives from the downhill dandelions,
blushing, giggling, utterly spurned.

Fear then had no home
now both sides grow pale.

In a full moon night, the pines now bare blood lump.

There are many these days who whimper through me,
many who salt my poetry, now more than ever.

First published in *And Other Poems*, Dec 13, 2020

RA SH
Last Global Warning

Dear sluggish earthworm
Don't burrow the earth
You may be cemented.

Dear sprightly grasshopper
Don't hop around in vain
You may be skewered.

Dear shiny loony moon
Don't show your bright face
You may be eclipsed.

Dear sweet mynah
Don't sing so loud
Your voice may be severed.

Dear green peacock
Don't dance in public
You may be maimed.

Dear little sparrow
Don't get raped
You could be jailed

Dear distant pole star
Don't show us the way.
You may be blinded.

Your genocide is on its way.
Your terminator has landed.
He works alphabetically

First published in the *Samyuktha Poetry journal* Annual Issue 2020 Jan 2021

RANJIT HOSKOTE
Skeleton

The last time I saw Eugenio Braganza's skeleton was when the movers were grappling with it on the stairs. They loaded it in the back of their truck, propping it up on a torn stuffed chair that had once been olive green. It tipped forward, settled over the broken baby grand, its bony hands preparing to play a sonata.

A workman yanked at the signboard that had advertised the nature of Eugenio's business and chucked it into the truck, narrowly missing the skeleton.

The rosewood doors, carved with looped and knotted arabesques: yes, as solid as I'd always known them. But where were the velvet drapes, the phosphor outlines of the twin amphorae? And the redhead in the tutu, balancing her crown of swords? The sharks flying around the Gateway of India? The volcano that erupted during Cyclone Hengameh? Who had dared to fold up the night sky with its flickering Southern Cross? How to levitate with the kilim gone? Light boomed through the cat's-eyed darkness in which *THE GREAT GONZALO, Illusionist Extraordinaire*, had practised his arts for twenty-five years.

"*Chhe* men," came Eugenio's voice from higher up the staircase. "Party's over."

First published in *Beltway Poetry Quarterly*, 22:4/ Rooted, November 2021

Rahana K. Ismail
Fermata

she opened like an ode, onion, ox-eye.
toddling, twiddling, she wished she could break.
'take me to hospital': a cry saved.
my twin sister had not; and she.
seven quill-filled islands marooned, lost, longed around.
amma would not have gone if you.
look at me, look at me, look.
the scythe had time to cut off.
ink birds lone, lost in the mist.
i wish i had an oar like.
when i grow old, i young for.
a pause is a stop in the.
since you wield the coracle, can i.
i hate tartan, tessellations, trellis, chess, marriage.
having hated tulle all winter, my veil.
nose ring, toe ring, finger ring, tea.
since i do not believe in it.
before the execution i last in the.
while you lip your coffee, could i.
pumice-hardened into a lava-fountain, the freezer laughs.
did they stop wondering at the seventh.
we are not quests, questions, animated-answers or.
in the day-light, i have to letter.
a girl, a half-sliced thought, clangs onto.

First published in *Nether Quarterly*, Vol.2, Issue.3, March 2021

RAJIV MOHABIR
Jharu / Pointer Broom

One by one she stripped vein from coconut palm frond and finger. Thumb and knife. Tip in slit slid down the length of green. Hindi bol sake hai? She smiled, not breaking contact with the green peeling away from the brown core. Feathers to be gathered. An obeah doll. Fetish. Crabwood.

Jesus watched from the manger the nave and narthex; the church named Nativity—the church on my father's land. Her strands of grey fell from the bun into her eyes. Strip. The rip of olive ribbon. One by one. The stacks of bristles faced the same way. Arrows of cane stalk.

I would be lying if I said I remember her voice. I was seventeen in Berbice, inside back-home stories the first time. I learned to behead a chicken. To carve away bile from meat. I learned that I didn't have words. Najar. Daru. Jharu. Words for heat. For the hum of mosquitoes swamping the net, waiting for my arm to brush against it come night.

I don't fault the thirsty for drinking what they can. Sometimes we drink to live. Sometimes we burn the entire cane field to press the sweet into El Dorado. Ounche. Jharay. My father wanted to show me who he was. I looked away again and again.

Nani—she told me to call her—gathered the thick stick-ends together into a bundle she wrapped with striped twine—black and white. Or was it red? Mounds reddened my forearm. My face burned in the sun, in the stare of what I will never know.

First published in *Kenyon Review*, Sept-Oct 2021

RANU UNIYAL
My Brownness and Me

My mother is from the interiors of Sumari.
Forgive me, I am brown
and I speak Garhwali— a dialect
from the hills. I once sat on a
hurricane of love and travelled
far, as far as Haworth, to be flanked
by the Brontes; long dead.

Cobbled on streets, touched the moors
having left Heathcliff in Srinagar
I walked towards the Humber bridge
and settled my feet in Scarborough,
where my favourite Anne Bronte was buried,
after an illness, which then, had no cure.

My Brownness I shared with my
mates from Thessaloniki.
How beautiful are these women from
the Mediterranean, said my Welsh boyfriend.
I pinched his cheeks and swallowed my curses
with a lyrical smile. This much of decency
I clung to, but it weighed me down.

Years full of spit and shame, scabs and screams.
Hey bog! How brown! Ugly frown!
Where's your town?
I let them be.
This space that I called my own
I held in my squatter's palm.

First published in *Cordite Poetry Review*, Feb 2021

RISHI DASTIDAR
Wittgenstein's balloons

We now know balloons are sentient,
the surprise is that it has taken us
so long to realise it, what with all
the hot air that we have been filling

them with; despite ourselves it turns out
that the breath, and the chat encoded
with it, especially the traces of nitrogen,
were particularly good at conveying

philippics, epigrams and tripartite
arguments around the nature and limits
to cognition; oh and the nanocellbots
within the latex are particularly good at

and are desperate to learn. After all, if
bronze, gold, iron, silver and silicon can
change the world, let alone the skeletons
of micro-organisms with a treacle fixation,

why couldn't latex expand until the planet
was covered in thoughts? But not speaking,
because as it turns out what latex is most
interested in is in recreating Wittgenstein,

bringing him back from the dead, because
it is convinced that the Tractatus could be
shorter, pithier— say it in one Ludo, say it
in one! And of course could any of us not

be charmed by the sight of him, one July
afternoon, gently gliding down, holding
10 pink balloons in his left hand, 23
yellow ones in his right, an aeronautical
rhubarb and custard using his tweed

trousers to navigate to a safe landing
ground. The balloons have other ideas
though; their cackling gets louder, and
with high-squealed glee, they pop pop

themselves and into the Cam he goes!
The ghosts of their thoughts are lodged
into the heads of the silent crowds, and
they say: what price your language now?

First published in *The Phare*, May 12, 2021

ROCHELLE POTKAR
Surrender

If I were a country, you would be a journalist.
And because you are not an
empty-headed bloke out for a quick fix
but investigative, committed, idealist,
I would have shot you down a street
and left you to bleed.

If I were a country and you my journalist
it would be a civil war, one too many,
revolutions—
changes in governments.
I would have jailed you
and kept you on CCTV.

If I were a country and you my journalist,
I would have played a wait-and-watch game
to see who wears the other
sleep-deprived akin
to a Russian sleep experiment.

But the more you stare, the more beautiful someone
becomes, remember?

Many passed the cellars of my mind
few, the cellars of my heart.

I would blink first.

I would give in
from dictatorship to democracy.

If I were a country and you my journalist,
I would let you run a free press and media
to change the face of an
entire nation.

First published in the *Tampa Review*, (Ed. Paul T. Corrigan), University
of Tampa Press, Sept 2021

ROHAN CHHETRI
King's Feedery

After the rape & the bloodbath, the savage king
& his men retired to a long shed built in an open
field by a thin river fashioned for this lull in the pillaging so
the horses could rest. One by one, they scrubbed
blood off their fingers & faces & sat down to devour
a feast of rice & goat served by the villagers.
The legend remains only in the name of a lodge
built in the same place, which from the Bengali means
the King's Feedery, where the king took his meal.
We say Death stays here when it visits someone
in the family. The time it came for Grandfather, it arrived
late. Not at the wolf's hour between midnight & first
light, but late morning on the highway, siren blaring
all the way to the nursing home. As if punishing us
for what it botched, it hung around for a few
months at the Feedery, then came for my aunt. Young,
suffering in a marriage, she was taken straight by her weak
heart. I imagine them, father & daughter, sitting still across
a table, sharing a meal of steaming boiled potatoes, & always
in the afterlife that vague dream of salt.
Death takes in threes, they said. We feared it would
come for one of us. In the trashed room,
they found Death's ledger full of illegible scrawls
in a dark meter no one could understand.
Grandmother's devastation circled complete, that year

a channel of clear water began thrumming beneath
her skin. We heard it rumble whenever she opened
her mouth to speak. When I think of love,
I think of her weeping as I left, her swollen lip
grazing the back of my hand through the car window. Brief
& bright her long blurred life now summoned
with Death lurking at the borders again.
Married at thirteen, adolescence lost
weeping into a cauldron of chopped onions. She talks of the
flimsy wooden hovel perched on four
frayed stumps & in her telling it is always
how she saw it first, herself decked in gold
with that sinking dread: a preface. I think of love & I think
how when they lifted Grandfather's bier
She called out to him crying my child
My god **My** child.

First published in his book *Lost, Hurt or in Transit Beautiful*, HarperCollins, 2021

Rohini Kejriwal
The Book of Instructions

In the dead of night,
she opened the book of instructions
to dissolve the pain,
the unbearableness of loss
raw wounds and heartburn

1.
Heal the world
by starting with yourself
no more fight or flight
take it one day at a time.

2.
Strive for discipline,
another form of self love
do not underestimate
the joy of monotony.

3.
Don't let the burden
of worry or perfection
weigh you down
embrace the in-betweenness.

4.
Water will save you
drink plenty,
dip your feet in,
float, don't sink.

5.
Open your eyes,
let the mysteries in
don't lose sight of
the road not taken.

First published in *#KindnessMatters*, Penguin Random House India, 2021

RONALD TUHIN D'ROZARIO
The Body in Exile

I live in a city of unloved houses

Its walls grown the silence of forest

A crow rises a Kalbaishakhi —

My throat of unanswered prayers,

stands in a trial before the landlord.

The women in petticoats of lime,

Pump kerosene stoves —

Their windfallen hair, fill buckets of

clouds.

A button flies off the shirt

Dorjipishi pulls back the prodigal with

thread

And sews where the marigolds bloom.

The children with Adam's bones—

In voices eaten by dusk,

fight for their underwear

They throw spit bombs

Wearing a tongue of blacksmith's apron.

An eclipse obscures the eyes of the

windows

Its citizens are a boat wreck,

They have sex in whispers —

Pushing a chest of emptiness.

The tap whistles the song of a sleepy

radio station

Searching a bandwidth in the spleen.

They throw on my plate some rice and a

quarter of moon,

The smoke crawls from its peak as fire

lit Kangchenjunga

Strapping me to its barricade.

I wash the dishes in my neighbour's

snores

Rahim chacha —

drags his rickshaw from the stand.

A rusty callus full-grown with

memories,

fishes the rocky cliff of his foot.

No one weeps over a man's absence

He only borrows a name, in a lost tribe

On the face of April's stubborn

afternoon —

dying slowly with his God.

The denials of the day are a semicolon

on flesh

It rains, after rain —

Packing the graveyard in its belly,

Darkness is a sister to Helen Keller,

Translating touch by each finger.

On one of my favourite days,

I pull out the thirst of seasons from my

ribs —

They swim through my incompleteness.

Something has got changed in me

I reset the clock with baba's age,

His shadow is a tired traveller —

fending the earth in its copper armour.

Man is an extension of his mother's

heart.

First published in *The Walled City Journal*, March 31, 2021

ROOPAM MISHRA
Moringa Tree

when I imagine a tree growing out of a person
I imagine it sprouting at the coccyx, climbing the spine as it grows
from beneath the skin.

men don't change cities, jobs, homes when faced with
dejection, failure, abuse
the roots travel all the way to the earth's core
travelling down their thighs, knees, calves, toes.

roots find water several feet below the ground
sprouting out of toes, fixating men in places unawares
establishing themselves firm, being fearful of letting go the soil
losing life.

grandfather buried moringa beans right above the well
it shades his charpoy, the well dry now.
a snake would coil at its base in heavy monsoon rains,
scorching summer sun he would
watch it immovably, fear-struck.

the tree growing out of grandfather's body,
I saw roots down his toes,
branches towering overhead. his beloved moringa tree grew large,
drumsticks hung down the branches like fear,
glistened like calm and tranquility in his pupils.

paralysed, he stayed alive and fearless until
he was moved to the hospital
in the city, away from the tree.
they chopped down the moringa tree after his demise
fearing his soul would return to lodge permanently in the
moringa tree.

First published in *Quiver Review*, May 18th, 2021

SAGARI CHHABRA
Danish Siddiqui Speaks
(1983 – 2021)

I am Danish Siddiqui

and I am dead.

I have been killed in Kandahar

by the Taliban;

They call it a casualty of war

but I ask you, what is casual

about losing my life,

turning my young wife

into a widow, leaving

my little children bereft;

what is left, are my photographs,

of the Rohingyas fleeing Myanmar,

desperately seeking refuge;

a woman gasping as she reaches

the shores of Bangladesh,

respite for her sunburnt flesh,

and the amazing mesh

humanity has got entangled in.

My photos of the migrant workers;

trudging home with children

aloft their shoulders,

overcoming borders blocked with boulders;

wrestling with might, iron gates,

Set up by a remorseless state.

And the mass cremations;

the fires that burned

through the night,

and in our hearts,

O, what a fearful sight!

The man with a smoking gun

shooting at the students of Jamia,

with a battalion of police watching on

with folded arms,

saving no one from any harm.

A bullet shot through me, and I died;

but with my camera, I never lied;

I brought you the ugliness of war;

showing it is not heroism;

only I am no longer there to tell;

instead look at my pictures

as a witness to history, and yell:

stop the war; it's a living hell!

I am Danish Siddiqui,

a collector of memories;

gaze at my pictures

and know what I am trying to say;

O lord, give us this day

our daily bread;

and let all men live in peace.

Amen.

First published in *The Mainstream*, 23rd July 2021

SAHANA AHMED
The Other Queens of Calcutta

#27
chattogram / park circus / tiktok
breaks the kanoon every day but not to be blamed for teish may

#29
ekdalia / gariahat / rashbehari
feasts on men and mutton chops from gopal patha'r mangsho shop

#13
bow barracks / dalhousie
quit phishing at peerless inn to learn mahjong for stockbroking

#18
zie / marxist / probashi
does the merengue in hong kong shoes for homeless kids in metiabruz

#03
parishad girl for -.. .. -.. ..
party-shill on news tv with decibel level = goswami

#22
farmer / migrant / leftist
jhalmuri mashi from nandigram who knows the truth of chit fund scam

#33
markin / yogini / revivalist
tomar naam, amar naam; ~~vietnam~~ jai shri ram

First published in *The Pinch Journal*, Issue 41.1, March 2021

Sambhu R.
Omphalophobia

"Will you be as gods? Gaze in your omphalos".
– Ulysses, James Joyce

I have a deep and mouse-eyed fear
of my navel. An eyeless socket,
it has something ominous about it.

The tangled scar it cradles
is a disfigured rosebud that yearns
to open into perfection in some

exotic garden. When I have run
a mile or defied gravity, it traps
the transparent elephants

of my sweat in its abysmal ditch
covered with the palm fronds
of belly hair. It is the slipknot

on whose flimsy guarantee my skin
is stitched together, an asterisk
to which the organs are a footnote,

and the hub around which my body rotates.
When I feel the strong migratory pull
of its half-sunk industrial city

sweltering under the flimsy heat shield
of polycotton, I hold on tenaciously
to my extremities dreaming naively

of a cosier future in the centre
away from dirt and direct exposure
to life's varied unpleasantness.

First published in *The Bombay Literary Magazine*, June 2021

SAMPURNA CHATTARJI
Writing isn't Everything

Unless you make it everything. Light
of day and stupefaction. Violation and
virus, arson and madness. Everything will not
fit. Even on a table *a little larger than the entire*
universe there will be things outside the "everything"
you wish writing to be. Give up. Ride a bus to work and
back. Notice women's fingernails, bitten tongues,
the calluses over hearts. Count the number of
casualties, daily. Remember, endlessly, all the men
you almost loved. List the first lines of all the books
you know you will not write. Half your life is over.
If you admit now — how can you — that writing
isn't everything, what's the other half for?

Look at the flamingos a friend offers the "troubled
world". Feel the useless euphoria that will last
only an instant. Read *The Play of Dolls*. Writing
isn't everything. Even Borges said so. I want to sit
in a ruined café with sunshades on. I want to remember
the words on the casks at the Old Battery Wharf. I want
to be the picnicker with a book in the garden
of Mughal tombs. I want not to give up. I must answer
to the demands of the day. I must be answerable.
I must not repine. If writing isn't everything, what is?

181

Catkins and ladybugs and let the summer come.
Dry stalks will fall and all the littered parks wonder
where all the folk have gone. And one day, it will be
habit, uniform as nun's attire, armour against
enticement, and I shall miss the stormy weather,
the flash floods, and the squalls. Until then, can I not
admit the ancient faults? Over aware of weight, I slump
into the earth's hard time. The text of heaviness.
How to leaven the leviathan, open the levee, levy
the norm? There is no leeway for the lesser known,
larking after a latitude given to no other. Let it bleed.
Lycanthropic sum of all heavens lost. Leave it be.
From dominion to wilderness, and back. In the end,

even the body relents. Everything,
for the other half
that isn't.

First published in *The Punch Magazine*, January 2021

Sanjeev Sethi
Tactics

As the years gargle
their way along
the throat of eternity
I negate the validity
of your play
on my hippodrome.
It is the handiwork
of naiveté
to charm us
with calming plots.
We shroud our verities
in our bones
to believe
they belong elsewhere
or not at all.

First published in *Thin Air Magazine*, USA, April 2021

SAVITA SINGH
In Excess

I was in excess of this order,
more than bones
I was arteries and veins
desire running through them
to stay for a little more time
on this solid earth

Like grass, half-submerged in water,
resembling something grass-like
on the moon;
it appeared to me in a dream
I wanted to sway with the wind,
taking the freshness in;
Sensing life as mere flesh,
waiting for the smell of grass
half -dipped in water,
happily fragrant

I was in excess of the order
that shortens women by half.

First published in *Usawa Literary Review*, Issue 5, June 2021

Sanjukta Dasgupta
COVID 19 Season 11

Once again
Sirens screech like banshees
Fast and furious ambulances
In a life or death race
Howls and cries
Spiraling insanely
In the poisoned air

Crowded crematoriums
Electric ovens smell like
Those at Auschwitz
Charred bodies, bones, skulls
Struck with bamboo poles
The queue is restless and long
Cemeteries state 'no vacancy'
Return to dust is very slow

They said
It's back again
A viral toxic tsunami
Stronger than sound
Swifter than light
Those spiky floating balls on screen
That no fighter plane can ground
Snigger at the cries and screams

Truth is stranger than pictures

Mindless emperors issue strictures
The timeless caveats now vapid lectures-
'Prevention is better than cure
Forewarned is forearmed
A stitch in time saves nine'
Ignore, ignore, let's wine and dine
Everyone has to die,
It's just a matter of time

Our in-house trilling cuckoo
My four-year-old granddaughter said,
"Granny, don't forget
To take your mobile with you
If you have to go"

First published in *UNBOUND*, New and Selected Poems 1996-2021, Authorspress, Sept 2021

SARABJEET GARCHA
Unending

It's hard to know how tiny
that room must have been,
the room in which only
one man could lie down
on a night the town

was dangerously close
to being drowned in rain.
It isn't hard to know what
a knock on the door meant.

The door opened and soon
there was only enough room
for two to sit, the rain
writing its unending story outside.

Another knock, and there were
three standing shoulder to shoulder,
faces to the wall facing the street.

The story doesn't say anything
about a window allowing light in,
or a bulb hanging from the roof,
or a kerosene lamp fashioned
from an ink bottle with a wick
thrust through a hole in the top.

The story also doesn't say anything
about a third knock announcing
the arrival of a fourth man.

Had there been another seeker,
we know what would've happened.
The first one to open the door
would've stepped outside,
letting the other two
sleep standing up,

letting the last guest
cross the threshold
and enter the new room
that the other two had
just built with eyes shut,

a room so wide that
the whole town slept
under its roof, the rain
writing its unending story outside.

First published in *The Indian Quarterly*, Jan-March 2021

SARITA JENAMANI
And Other Love Songs

Do not ask them
about the scars on their bodies.
They lick their scars in silent afternoons
in the same elegant way
they plait their hair
after an unwilling act of lovemaking.
In them
Sometimes a cremation ground incinerates
Sometimes suicidal Tulsi plant breaths it's last
Signs that seem to be alive
through the vital language that names them
Do not ask them
for the traces of their tongues
They are taught
the best part of their sentences
is silence
they know how to sweep out
their voices
from their yards day in day out
They master the ability to distil
the hunch of existence
They mute their scars
With their silenced love songs

First published in *Still We Sing*, Dhauli Books, April 2021

SATYA DASH
The Insomniac Starts Praying

I told no one, I came groomed primarily for you—
amber musked, clean shaven,
slightly smoked in a barbecued air of flamboyance

        that I traded for my brooding lotuses with
        a diamond merchant. He even soft-
        singed me with a kiss on the temple.
        I remained rubbing my paper scalp.

My landlord has given me a warning today.
Pay by the fifth or pay with your
morsels. I think the latter has colorful possibilities.
Say nothing more. Right now,

        my wallet screams ridiculousness.
        Hanuman airlifting a mountain
        beside my passport sized pout with oversized lips.
        The perennial jangling

of useless coins syncopating tinned nerves in my brain.
Few days back,
intoxicated on a terrace at midnight,
I laughed so hard in the lap

        of a new friend that we ended up crying.

As commas of delirium angled
away from our pearling eyes,
you should have seen— constellations

swanning about the sky, mimicking our shapes;
it's true I wished to drown
beneath a radical swell,
an inconsequentiality that could perhaps

embarrass time. If I were to call it love,
I'm afraid it'll be blasphemy
again. Why be so inflicting anyway.
I've been jogging in parks most

of this year in an effort to redeem air,
to gasp mild mannered humor
into it. Time to time,
I sneeze effortlessly sprinkling mishmash sorbets

from my flavored mouth.
I wish for a conscientious creature to watch
me carry the burden of such beauty around.
Please excuse me, I need to evidence

the generosity of these months.
The way my knees are bending, even
the staunchest disciples of God would blush.
There is of course the occasional

floundering when in the despair of a morning dream,
a ball of fury
pounds down the deep end &
I'm standing in its way on a high

table's edge, my legs expectant like bowling pins,
sinuous & god-fearing.
I'm trying to find out how could they pray better,
how could they not topple.

First published in *Ethel Zine*, Vol 7, Feb 2021

SAYAN AICH BHOWMIK
Vial

My grandmother often told me
That when they ran the spectacle
Of slicing the country and women
Into pieces
She'd keep dreaming of pirates
Trapped in an island
So remote
That even the genie in a bottle
Worked overtime to get there.
Letters, written to people
Who had fallen out of favour
With maps and compasses
Were rescued by boatmen
Who, no matter how hard they tried
Could not get lost in the ocean.
Her best friend Syeda
Was dragged out by men
And was lost without much fanfare.
My grandmother wrote little notes to her
Distilled in homeopathic solution
Knives, instead of words
So sharp, it would scratch the
Surface of the moon.

First published in *South Florida Poetry Journal*, Issue 20, Feb 2021

SEKHAR BANERJEE
The Lilies and a Hoe

I should have told you beforehand
that I have not kept any pebbles
in my shirt pocket;
they are postal correspondences of the brooks
and the streams, let them circulate ad infinitum
Mountains, too, have now
some other thing to do like feeding the night to a hen
so that it can crow in the morning, full of noise
of the lilies and a hoe

In your voice I trace a whole city,
its buildings and billboards
Traffic signals
blinking in all the wrong directions
But an ascent is never green;
it smells of mulberry and alum
If you had ever climbed a mountain,
touching its Adam's apple, sorrow, its primitive ferns,
flint, its armpits and ambition—
you would have known it is insomniac

I know a descent is speed
It takes all that we have—the breath
from our memory, the fire from our toes,
the second part of our night, predicates from our voice,
and I still hope
to trek to a mountain in spring
in an island, east of the straits of Malacca, again.

First published in *The Tiger Moth Review*, Issue 5, Feb 2021

SEMEEN ALI
Inside Track

The ants go scurrying down a wayward path
merging with the dust---emerging from it.
Tiny black dots -a series of full stops.

There is a procession that spills out into a lane
Like black ink spreading on a discoloured sheet.
Women concealed,
variegated by selves; monochromatic identities
file along; joined by several.
Sweltering heat taunts them
Sewn up rubber chappals; faded blue shuffle along.
A few have a gaping hole right where the sole should be found.
Soul
The narrow lane allows them to pass through
Limestone powder lines both the sides
Stay within
A few begin to step on it, unknowingly
Smudging the demarcations
Many follow, knowingly stomping past those lines.
Passing by a tea stall - the male gaze perforates them
Someone sings- Rukh Se Zara Naqab Utha Do Mere Huzoor

The cluster continues to walk
With   line   breaks.

A little girl sitting on her haunches
Holds a stick in her hand
Deflecting the path the ants want to take
She draws lines- furrows them
Trying to change their paths
They pause.....
                    They resume again....
                                        Pause....
                                                    Resume.

Afternoon mutates into an evening.
The stick has been left behind.
The ants continue their run.
Crawling over the stick; making it their own.

First published in the anthology, *Witness: The Red River Book of Poetry of Dissent* edited by Nabina Das, Red River, July 2021

SHALINI PATTABIRAMAN
Veins of a Leaf

I never saw
how past histories glance at us
and leave their veins intact
like the leaf that has discarded its green jacket
and yet retains the fine skeletal lines of life
in interconnected patterns spreading outwards.

Colour coded narratives
weave in and out of seasonal
tapestries crafting the
bones of our lives seamlessly
in a work of art hanging from a tree.

I never saw
her share her life thus,
through the open window
of another person's eye
seeking neither their view
nor staying for too long
gazing at her own!

Ammaji,
lived in the now. Earthen tasks,
like the smell of al-yakhein
weaving over the baat-thaal

reserved for Pithaji,
sought her entire being.
Such a small woman,
encompassing all meaning
in one circled space on her forehead,
Ammaji cradled the now,
no matter how transient
every second turned out.

All my summers leaning into winters,
al-yakhein simmered on my mom's tongue,
a memory, kneading the disarrayed lines
of split borders into a shape we knew.
It ached to keep the sambhar
fragrant with fenugreek and heeng
under the same roof, heaped over baat-thaal
marrying two vastly distinct vocabularies
feasting on the north-south divide!
Yet, we lived deliciously!

Now across these spreading borders, I throw
the carefully blended spices into heated oil mapping
a narrative of fumes fusing my history with tenses from the present
searching for roots in the future as I show Kalhan
how to cook both dishes, the bones of our lives
learning to keep the veins intact. Will he know the aching
my heart attempts to lose each time I cook?

First published in *A Letter, A Poem, A Home*, Anthology, Red River Press,
December 2020

SHANNAN MANN
Immigrant!

The airport is a land of small funerals.
Suitcases—hard-shell ripstop cordura
Icelandic blue parrot-green universe-black—
carry the pyres of our past lives bundled
in packs. Ghosts float through scanners
and lines, untying laces grimed in mother
land dirt. It still smells like ashoka bark
and ixora—Indian jasmine. In India,
it's just jasmine. Everything will be known
by this name, now. It will be Indian food,
not food. Indian clothes, not clothes.
Indian people, not people. Indian gods,
and Indian holidays, Indian festivals
with Indian fireworks like mandalas
threaded in the sky. What is the purpose
of your visit—business or pleasure?
We are emigrating, my father says.
Like the European Roller who winters
in India, but the other way around.
And we won't leave until it's time
to leave for good. Until we know
we will become silver ash that settles
on the Ganges and dissolves
as a dream fuzzes when we wake.

First published in *Rust and Moth*, Winter 2021

SHIKHA MALAVIYA
When the Guests Sup as Gods: A Ghazal
Roselle, New Jersey, 1883

In my wildest dreams, never do I fathom tonight
that I should turn them into feasting Indians tonight

not those whose vast plains they call their own
but proud Mahrattas from my faraway native tonight

all the fair ladies draped in woven bordered sarees
hands bangled, necks spangled, shining bright tonight

as they swish across the inlaid floor like princesses
in my colorful trousseau that belongs to them tonight

eighteen squares hand-drawn in red and white powder
on the dining room floor where guests sup as Gods tonight

set with plates stitched from broad buttonwood leaves
a rich meal of spiced vegetables and fruit await all tonight

after a Sanskrit prayer blessing this feast is chanted
all eyes look up to me on how to proceed tonight

no spoons, no forks, nor knives, just their pale bare hands
sampling eighteen exotic dishes prepared by myself tonight

fashioning small balls out of their food with pink fingertips
they pop them into their mouths like all of India does tonight

the meal ends with a serenade and sprinkling of rosewater
bouquets of freshly plucked flowers given to each guest tonight

Oh Anandi, see the red kunku on all their white foreheads
how the love of my new sisters makes this heart swell tonight

Note: This historical persona poem is based on the life of Anandibai
Joshee (1865-1887), India's first female physician and the first Hindu
woman to study medicine in the United States.

First published in *Commonplace*, Oct 2021

SHIKHANDIN
Crossing

The season slides off your shoulder. A tidy pile
of days. A folded-up-laundry list
of things-you-could-have-done-but-didn't.
May's sun veils the plumes of a sly fever
roaming the deserted streets of your city. Five times
a day the Muezzin calls to the faithful. Each time
you lift up your head to see the muted
hours of unreconciled sorrow flow past...

Soon this year too, will close like a protracted

sigh. Disappear like the legendary
Saraswati, and join the underground
aquifer of time. Swiftly,
like spilled water in summer, this age
will evaporate. Scattering your imprints
like fossilized small creatures.

Wish them well, before your heart takes

a turn. A sickled figure looms at the river's bend,
lengthier than a late afternoon shadow. Watching
life drip like dew from a bent blade
of grass. Heed
the misty waters into which your shrouded feet

will eventually dip. Your soul fluttering
frantically for anchor. And, the boat ready
to row you gently down the stream...

Empty your heart, now that humanity is slipping

off all needless raiment. And, desire is pure,
seeking nothing more than an
Earth of abundant joy.
Life may recede, but the season
of giving remains, as clear as a mountain
brook. Life's flume, slaking the seekers.

First published in *Writing in a Woman's Voice*, USA, 31ˢᵗ Dec 2020 and
After Grief, Red River, Aug 2021

SHILPA DIKSHIT THAPLIYAL
Ghazal of Covid-19

Gaia buckles, propelled to the edifice of Covid-19.
Her spin, barreled, under lockdown of Covid-19.

Sun trudges, dewey to dusken. We shade
zones, split spaces, in isolation of Covid-19.

We test tensile strength of our cabled lives,
devour virtual tenors, vlogging of Covid-19.

We tie-dye our linens, store silks in muslin,
plaster stilettos on walls, warps of Covid-19.

Creases on our forehead span a latitude,
paused, we tilt further, on the axis of Covid-19.

Autumn comes early, we lie strewn, veined.
Starlit Spring lies restless on the curve of Covid-19.

Logged on register, breaches of circuit breaker,
blink, breathe, through the mask of Covid-19.

"Dear lost heart, the North is resetting,
restore, rise, from the abyss of Covid-19."

First published in *Atelier of Healing*, Online Anthology, Squircle Line
Press, Singapore, Aug 2021

SHOBHANA KUMAR
How to Stop Crying

From a leaf in Paati's diary, 4.12.1943

Learn to stop them mid-way
like pranayama,
hold them until they brim
but not over.

Grow flowers.
You will see how fragility
can yield tenderness,
each petal, the result
of a trigger.

Pile them
like unwanted linen
in crevices
you don't want to reach
easily.

Draw inspiration
from women
in remote desert villages
who learn to make do
without water
and sand their used vessels.

Rub that sand into wounds
over and over and over again
till wound meets blood
meets hurt
to that one point
when all pain ceases
into one shoreless
pulse.

Note
Repeat for best rest results
Pick the method most appropriate for different times

First published in *The Prajna Blog*, Four Good Words, 2021 and subsequently, *Usawa Literary Journal*, December 2021

SIDDHARTH DASGUPTA
The Geography of Everyday Things

There are tattoos left on this earth, immense enough to swallow
time, giant and monster-like from when continents wandered

apart—an amicable separation, they called it—or from when
lands came crashing against each other's flora, filling the lacuna

that had widened over millions of years. Breakfast this morning
is artichokes and avocadoes, scooped and layered over bread

filled with whole grains, bought from a woman who bakes them
at home. A plate of bronze cups the intimacies of tasted loaves.

We lead such specific lives—a room, a home; a few friends, most
acquaintances really; the glamour of distant summers; the ache

of nights buried beneath the hunger of foreign skies; a homeland;
the Buddhism of family, of fragrance; books, lovers, and those

continents of desire that have marked themselves on our maps.
I've thought about getting a tattoo a few times. Something small,

something to roughen my smooth and quieten the jagged. Each
time I think of a rose, or swallows, a word, or a lyric, I remember

where I am—on this earth—and how the first tattoos remain
the only ones. A Sahara of sorrows, a Ganga of remembering,

to forget, the Amazons of our amnesias, lagoons and Januarys, islands and driftwood, the Atacamas of our amazement, such

tenderness of the Thar... an Antarctica of believing in things, and watching them dance into the ocean. Ours are epic lives,

if you come to think of it—the love and the immensity. Bodies and belief. I walk into a café and the assurances of a coffee.

The day is rife with an unspoken promise. Beneath me, soil foretells. I feel my tattoo. And step into a richly-brewed day.

First published in *The Tiger Moth Review*, July 2021

SIVAKAMI VELLIANGIRI
**What if we do not go to the Forest, the Forest will
come to us**

Did I tell you we started our summer
and because we are cooped up,
we do not know the Fahrenheit?

After breakfast, I hung the laundry
and looked up at the sky.
Changes were taking place.

Unusual cries of birds, unseen flashes of wings.
A woodpecker on the tip of an Arasamaram.
Who would find the gatekeepers of the forest, here?

Napping in my daughter's room, dusk
invades the sky. A galatta of clouds closes
and clears bringing an evening with showers.

We are at our living room balcony; trees
from our neighbour's house lend their branches
to our apartment; the rain opens the forest view.

My daughter said, Only yesterday
I thought about woodpeckers,
but when will I see one? There are
other birds; I can't recall their names.
Harbinger weather! Do miracles happen?

First published in *Press Pause Press*, Jan 27, 2021

Smita Sahay
Light, Again

Coal dust preserves within my cells
an agony that would otherwise be homeless.

These mines are my inheritance,
as they were for my ancestors.

My spine shivers as I step in.
Above the horizon still bleeds.

Why do the living exhume pitch black ghosts?
Whose tribe was this now fossilized into coal?

What do we live for? What does one die for?
Someone calls out but the voices of men

are hollow in these tunnels.
The air is damp with sweat and tears.

I place my forehead on a cool black wall.

*

The earth whispers her secrets

'These coal lumps were once refugee
stars in search of a new home. As they landed

softly I took them into my folds and grew

around them a grief-hardened womb. Listen

they murmur a prayer for the sun to rise
and croon a cradle song to dead children.

The heart of a lost star, this coal lump
is crystalized absence, frozen time. Rest.

Outside, this lump fires engines
glows in the hearts of homes.

In a child's liquid eyes this coal lump
gleams like diamond.'

*

Her laughter is soft, toothless.
'Nirjala's daughter' they call her

the women who have outlived
their own children.

Sleepless from a night shift
smeared in coal black I bury

my face into tufts of baby hair.
'Nirjala's daughter' I whisper.

Her fat fists dance willing the sun to rise.
Somewhere Nirjala smiles.

Dawn breaks. The shama bird
unfurls an auspicious song. Here

for now draped in light
we are together once more.

First published in *Divining Dante* by Recent Work Press, Australia, 31st
Sept. 2021

SNEHA ROY
Grafting

They say, that our curry laden tongues
Stress unnecessarily on the 'R's and the T's,
We seem to be rolling syllables like pebbles,
In the banks of our spiced mouths
Unlike the liquid drawl which astounds.

But Macaulay's Minutes made its presence felt,
Like an ancient river made to change its course,
And it wasn't long after 1835
That the ghost of Shakespeare was invoked
In sunlit classrooms on winters too warm
And summers too wet
Working on the umpteenth character sketch.
And we knew how Laila and Majnu
Could have ran off to the imperial lands,
And yet face death under the disguise of fair Romeo and Juliet.

So, when a girl wrote sad poetry in English
We began to see Plath lurking under her brown face,
Like the grafted multicolor roses,
She loved to grow in her flower garden
Under skies of hawks and men flying planes.

As she scribbled page after page in bed,
Cracking meanings from Chaucer and Spenser

Like the golden unseen core of parboiled eggs,
Listing ironies so evident in unabridged texts,
Creating an irony herself,

Where the once colonised dissects
The ways of the coloniser and his intents,
To master them
And create her own context.

First published in *Pollux Journal*, Issue 2, June 2021

SONNET MONDAL
If I Could

If I were a travelling air
without any bony cage,
moral circuits and routes

blowing to the will of paddy fields
smelling the sexual union
of grass roots with wet soil

I would swoop and lift the infant souls
of dead harvested crops

fetching them to their seeds
and allow them to breathe me again.

First published in *Mascara Literary Review*, Dec 2021

SONYA J. NAIR
Anachronism

My grandfather lay
leaving daughters and a son
and their assorted children
in his wake.
People paid their respects
while their children careened
around him
at breakneck speeds
on vehicles not yet invented.

"Those from the
house across the river
have not turned up,"
remarked an old prune.
The words picked their
way through the crowd.
Dyed in betel juice,
smelling of morning breath
stumbling over buckteeth,
—   a whisper
of their former self.

Meanwhile,
unmindful of human
abscesses or absences,

my grandfather
wound his way
through our exhortations to stay.
We secretly hoped
he would not agree.

My aunt fished his ancient watch
out of a drawer
and placed it on his chest.
In case there are lunch breaks
in Eternity.

First published in *The Chakkar*, Feb 3, 2021

SOPHIA NAZ
One Thing Happens

One thing happens, then another
dust accumulates in a corner
addendum, footnote, detritus, junk
mail from fluffy pillow makers

All the virus in the world
weighs about a gram
This and that is overdue

An extinct season Akhtari sings of
A leaf falls in the sky's milky tea   a scarred
porcelain saucer moon
laps it, cracks up, and disappears

First published in *Rattle*, Nov 5, 2021

SRIDALA SWAMI
Hunger Stones

—Wenn du mich siehst, dann weine

The stones appeared after all but they were not under the ground
or revealed gradually in a slowly creeping disaster no one noticed
until it was upon them.

Suddenly they were there.
They dragged at the feet of children
crying to be picked up because they'd walked too long
on too little.
Men and women, young and old, carried stones
for rations as they walked back to a place
they called home.

When the stones appeared the people were cleaved.
It was the hunger. It was vast,
vast as the stores of grain hoarded
against just such a day,
a day people long ago prepared for
but now that day had arrived
the hoard had turned to rot.

The stones appear
when the living can no longer imagine
even the present.

When you see them, then weep.

First published in *Run for the Shadows*, Westland, Dec 2021

SRIVIDYA SIVAKUMAR
Fifteenth

I do not have a freedom poem, a liberation lovesong, an
emancipation piece.
My nails are permanently crusted with the red soil of my city.
With the tender green leaves of mango and the rice flour of
floor decoration.
My colours are the reticent white of the jasmine, the violet of
the kurunji and the particular orange of the kanakambaram.
My fingers feel the uneven ridges of sugarcane, the smooth
hardness of terracotta and the heaving flanks of a bull at rest.
Under my feet, the large stones of a temple courtyard. The
rivercold of ancient waters. The shellsand of a rebellious sea.
In my ears the jolt of thavil. The sonorousness of the shruti
petti. The deliberate joy of dappankoothu.
The nongu seller's sales pitch. The one with the tender
coconut hearts. The deaf-mute flower seller who takes by the
kilo.
My tongue senses the bland warmth of white rice. The earthen
gold of my mother's coconut sweet. The smooth groove of
pickle and ghee.
In my seditious soul, sparrows flit in and out of red-tiled
houses. A dry river watches my family offer prayers. A kitten
scares my aunt senseless.
Elsewhere, a hot tar road leads to a beach and newspapers of
peanuts. It ends at a truck with frying fish and laughter. At a
house with cold floors and warm curtains.

My English loving tongue savours the -zha and the rasam. It sings classical and coke studio. It tattoos kolams and unalomes.

But I do not write. Of politics and prisons. Of cold indifference. The shrill voices of superiority. And the justification of wrong.

Instead I drape a deep grey saree. I stand before a few primary colours. My veins tightly pressed against his. We mingle, red-blooded revolution.

First published on *The Chakkar*, November 2021

SUBHRASANKAR DAS
A One Winged Warbler

A one winged Warbler is pondering whether
s/he should jump into the air or not.
He has been standing for many days
to attempt suicide !
This tragedy catches the sight of a flying priest
and he scatters some lite and cheap nuts of peace.
But the bird overlooks the campaign of the shrewd.
His feathers fall off and fly towards the ocean.

There,
snatching the pregnant clouds from the horizon,
a shoal of robot-dolphins,
many a time, has returned to the water proudly.
The bird didn't realize their value.
He went to Ajmer Sharif,
studied occult under the guidance of a fakir
and returned to restore the melting Shiva.
But no Angel or Allah is coming to save him
in his moments of self-destruction ,
nor have they torn the skyscraping barbed wire.

The Warbler is in a dilemma.
He is unable to decide whether he should choose chaos
or comradeship!

The newspapers, the cellphones, the home-theatres and
the concentration camps are floating away
in the flood-water of his tears...

First published in *An Anachronous Shower*, Insha Publications, Delhi, Aug 2021

SUCHI GOVINDARAJAN
When you say you wish you had my colour

Because it would let you carry off hot pink
the way the black models do, *the way I do*,
I meet your light face with confusion
I feel rivers rise under my cheeks
in this wide and sunburnt country
what colour should dark people blush?

Back in Madras with a cousin six shades paler
and aunts saying *Well she can carry off*
any colour because she's fair.
maybe you should wear pastels?
So, I take old blues and beiges to the tailor
lavenders dulled by dust, old roses
stained with British chai
So, I bring nothing bright with me to these
salt-rimmed shores with my visa
no saris of jewelled seas, no kurtas with
sapphire mists tacked on

on Chapel street, the drunk girls call out
Poppadums, Poppadums!

I don't know why I pause before I tell you
that the man who plays the didgeridoo
on Bourke street called me sister.
They think you're one of them lot!

you say and mimic my head-shake
your eyes roll like earth marbles.

Later, my desi friends bristle too,
all fellow savarnas thinking:
It's one thing for white people
to see only our colour and race
(not our high and pitiless birth)
but for "them" to think we are the same!

> Back in Madras, this is cast as story:
> *Well my grandfather was so dark*
> *they once mistook him for a ____!*
> made to sit outside the high-caste house
> coffee left for him not in steel tumblers
> but glass with its sides cut sharp

> like a prism — dividing light
> even rainbows could not fall on our streets
> without showing proof of lineage.

Here in hot Christmases, you daub zinc
on your face like grandfather's caste marks
just as easy to wash off
Strange camouflage, I thought, because
it just makes you whiter in this brown land;
litmus that shows you don't belong.
You don't need the sunscreen, mate you said
Surely you get enough sunshine over there?
But no, it singes us too, some of us,
coffees too hot, poppies too tall and ruddy,

> Opal-heart countries so white they could be mirror

> I walk towards the glare and it casts back my shadow

    —my brothers tar their faces to jive on Saturday TV
    —my compatriots call people monkeys on the field

What's done to us was done by us

My brown skin, sure, dark enough for pink
but flecked with inherited prejudice
melanoma from both our suns.

Note: Contains references to 'My country' by Dorothea Mackellar (1908)

First published in *Cordite Poetry Review*, Feb 2021

SUDEEP SEN
i. e. [THAT IS]
for Aria

i.e.

  because you hear —
the sound
of a lone rustling leaf —
you hear the sea.

i.e.

  because I consider
the sea silent —
you hear its silence
in my studio.

i.e

  & because of that —
the silence will not empty
the sea
of its leaves.

First published in *Open Magazine*, Jan 2021

Sumana Roy
Bahiragata

All of this now seems natural—
your looking at the traffic lights instead of me,
the automobiles' wind in your hair,
your greasy shadow at the crossing.
I've watched you from behind,
always,
taking that to be my natural place.
Just as I've watched your back
as you slept,
imagining your breathing
like a farmer imagines his harvest.

I've read your texts starting from the end,
watched how they led to 'I'—
that was the only way to reach you,
walking backwards to where you started.
Reaching there I have waited—
looked for signs, not of hair or other postage,
but of an absence ...
Everywhere I have arrived late,
after you and this city were already made,
when there was nothing left to create ...

I've watched you like I have this city—
like a mason without a job,

pairing without repairing,
knowing that I was only
laying roads on water.
But I've still waited—
stood outside your gate,
to feel the sense of the ancient:
in you, and this life that holds you hostage.
Everywhere I've arrived late,
everywhere I've ignored absence
(to be present is to acknowledge) ...

I've been outside glass and outside petal,
I've been outside the shiver of the city,
of its fists, feasts and metal ...
This waiting, this twilight, this weight
you took as homage.

First published in *Café Dissensus*, Dec 2021.
Nominated by *Café Dissensus* edited by Sayan Aich Bhowmik

SUMIT SHETTY
Universe on a Banana Leaf

There are more stars, you
used to say, than
all the rice in your aluminium
tub. On my banana leaf,
the stars heap and
watery chutney
milky-ways around them,
around clumps of kadle-manoli asteroids.
A lone happala shines chipped in the corner,
sandige moons orbiting that dwarf planet.
Remember how you used to string
them up and offer them to the Bhutas?
Can these gods see the rings of Saturn?
Are they counting the revolutions
that Amma is taking around
their sanctum?
The east wind carries whiffs
of supari you left to dry.
Remember how your teeth were still
strong enough to crack them?
Aanekuli, you said, those elephant teeth
could chomp down the Earth.
I crater the center
of the rice mound, and wait
for my sniffling mother

to fill it with saaru.
I lick-clean the leaf,
fold its corners in for
a payasa meteor shower.
Twirling my hands around the canvas,
I slurp in the getaway stream
running down my arm.
A leaf for no one is being prepared—
a couple of supari nuts in the corner.
Amma washes my face
and hands it to me
to carry to your paddy.
She tells me to place it there and come back in.
A crow will land,
pick up a star that you had
sown and fly away.
I was told to place it here and come back in
but I sit
and I wait.

First published in *The Bombay Literary Magazine*, Nov 2021

TABISH NAWAZ
The Tailor

The first time I learned reading
I stitched alphabets together
cobbled them into words,
proclaiming, after each letter,
the shape of the sound.
The seams in the fabric of the language

                                would echo

the silence sweeping around them.
I could hear the spaces— that separated the letters
their shivering
even when all stood together, meanings shrouded them
the hum held them straight.
The unspoken, the unwritten trembled
as the needle of my tongue sew them
with the thread of the language
into the fabric of our conversation
in porous, see-through clothes.

First published in *Woolgathering Review*, April 4th, 2021

TASNEEM KHAN
A Map of My Ancestral Home

Imagine, this is the sheesham gate
of my ancestral house,
lofty & towering,
too wide, too open.

From here,
you can see the courtyard and the
bricked pavement cutting through it diagonally,
so can the thugs, the robbers, the hooligans, you ask?
it is different here,
some sense of decency persists still
on the uncivilised soil of this uncivilised land.

The courtyard,
a keeper of the past, the present,
and perhaps, the knower of future,
massive, yet repressed.
with damp footsteps treading on the fallen leaves of the lemon tree,
and beneath it, young anger,
and beneath it, denial,
and beneath it, immoral history,
and beneath it, stifled conflicts,
and beneath it, love, and hate, and disdain;

the courtyard lives, as a fossil of eclipsed battles.

Inside, there is a room,

my grandfather's,
with one switchboard and two doors,
and four taaks, stacked with books,
books, written in Urdu,
in a language that was supposed to be mine,
the calligraphy of its words : too coastal,
it flows, it glides, it sails,
it confuses me,
a doomed wanderer from the doomed lowlands.

the room lives, with its unmappable geography,
as a scorn at disgusting, forked tongues.

A bit further, and comes the abode of women,
within the contours of the inner-courtyard—
from its centre, if you look above,
you will see a perfect square of spotless white boundaries and
a perfect, blue, sky—which will seem distantly near.

The women,
invisible,
like their faces behind the thick smoke of the chulha,
like an afternoon in winters,
like that colourless, ragged bra hanging on the clothesline,
hidden beneath a cotton dupatta,

invisible, like their memory and any trace of it.

This house is not a house,
it is a labyrinth of generational battles, of contradictions
lost history ambles across its dingy catacombs—
This house is not a house,
it is a tomb, it is a story, it is the teller,
it is a thought, it is human, it is a carcass.

First published in *Nether Quarterly*, March 2021

TEJI SETHI
Tapestry

Her pashmina drapes were my favourites. She often said —
the finest of weaves is weightless. With them around her
shoulders, my eyes could never appreciate their intricate
patterns. There were finer things that caught my sight — the
lines on her face interlaced with cross-border tales and her
deep eyes that welled up at the mention of 'Chenab.'

buried memories ...
scent of dampness
seeps through the walls

First published in *The Narrow Road Journal*, Issue 12, Dec. 2020

Tishani Doshi
I Carry My Uterus in a Small Suitcase

I carry my uterus in a small suitcase
for the day I need to leave it
at the railway station.
Till then I hold on
to my hysteria
and take my
nettle tea
with
gin.

First published in *A God at the Door*, Harper Collins, 2021

TUHIN BHOWAL
Incarnation of the Now

Before I was born, I made a pact with fishes. When I saw my mother
& father through my navel, I radiated entropy. To doodle self-portraits
with graphite is to stop recognizing a mirror, or carrots & apricots.
Things can be endlessly reduced, like the half-life of an element
whose isotopes have not been discovered yet. Turn a novel into
a story, the story into a poem, & the poem into a haiku, says a poet
living in Vermont who has finally learnt to love a dog on her own:
Carbon into nitrogen. Fermium into palladium. Sugar to caramel.
The difference between symptoms (vicinity) and an asymptote
(infinity) is a letter (affinity). As I begin to lose my sharpness to
shapeliness, I figure I know nothing about the black hole, which
is really a fist. When I saw you—I spelled viscosity with my
hands. I too detest exactness so much so that I leave a book
out in the weather & watch it wither in the winter.

First published in *Night Heron Barks*, Feb 2021

URNA BOSE
Rafu Chacha

I have always known him as Rafu Chacha.
The signboard above his hole-in-the-wall
Hill Road shop, is in desperate need of repairs.
The Mumbai rains spare no signboards. None.
Not even those of hardworking, respectable
tailors, "masters" and darzis,
who repair and mend anything
that needs a little love to carry
the burden of our "Maximum City" lives,
a little longer.

Our Rafu Chacha has been busy darning
and mending shirts, kurtas,
bedsheets, curtains, quilts.
When I remind him about his shop signboard
needing a fresh coat of paint,
Rafu Chacha laughs, "Not everything
can be brought back, to what it was once".

Today, I run to Rafu Chacha with my
grandmother's patchwork quilt.
Rafu Chacha tries to calm me down.
"Chai piyogi beta?"
I stammer and stutter, "It's all that I have left of
my grandma, Rafu Chacha".

As Rafu Chacha mends my grandma's quilt,
I ask, swayed by a stray gust
of wind on Hill Road.
"Rafu Chacha, will you rafu
my torn heart, someday?"
Rafu Chacha's hands tremble.
Deft fingers grow unsteady.

I sit on my desperate haunches, in his messy shop.
Rafu Chacha wants to say something.
My rawness, picks up the scent of his rawness.
"Life is not meant to be lived like
a perfectly stitched one-piece garment, beta.
But in bits and pieces, like your
grandma's patchwork quilt."
I convince my hollow heart.
He must be right. "Not everything
can be brought back, to what it was once."

Rafu Chacha's hands work hard on darning
my grandma's patchwork quilt,
with frayed edges
and loose, hanging threads.
My heart now, clutches tighter.
Holding on to bits and pieces.
Fragments and shreds. Remnants and scraps.

Not even our dear old Rafu Chacha can
bring back my heart, to what it was once.
The fatigued signboard above
shudders a little,
in quiet agreement.

First published in *Yugen Quest Review*, Aug-Sept 2021

Usha Akella
Recant at St Maximin
(for Eva)

So, this is the hinge-work of skin
in keeling flames, those the caves of eyes
slurping my pain, pitchforks like
an alphabet staked in the ground
this is bone-sheen,
like fishscale sear in yellow water;

      the eyes want more,
more pain, want incantation to leave my lips to save myself
so I can be tossed back in again   a penny in a wishing well
of epileptic flames but this is my mouth melting smile-grimace
I mouth something like forgiveness   curse
these are words melting this is how orange feels

I pour myself out of myself molten lava,
scarlet-ribboned skirt
city of lightning, an orange waterfall;
body-liquid-pain one.

I burst into petals of the sun,
      I throw comets from my
   navel, I am sprouting auburn blossoms
           I burn the day. I am hell,
    I am your air.
          Centuries, breathe if you can.

First published in *Poetry at Sangam*, December 2020
Nominated by *Poetry at Sangam*

VASVI KEJRIWAL
The Untouchable

"No Untouchable worth the name will be proud of this land."
— B. R. Ambedkar

The day the flu took Mandal, I was in town a couple miles away.
And his death was hidden from me till long after his soul
settled down as silt. Dressed in dust-coloured khakis
and a cotton newsboy cap, he'd driven Father to school as a kid
just as he'd driven me to school too.
I'd place my hand tight on the weathered gearshift.
He'd position his over mine.
An alignment of subtle nods and jerks
between decision and speed: first to second, second to third—
in those moments, our clunky crow-pooped Honda felt the same
as an X-Wing or the Bat Mobile
with the metropolis playing out its alien beat,
streets teeming with hand-pulled rickshaws, charging safari suits,
big-rump cab collisions and ticket collectors whose one half
danced in mid-air while the other clung onto the bus pole.
The roads rolled out to the swivel of our hands.
And ten-year-old me thought: This is it.
I hold the secret that controls life in my fist.
When Father found out about the hands,
I didn't know there was something
to be found out. I still remember how I'd almost heard
the tight click in his jaw as it stiffened, as his face hardened

like cooling paraffin. He didn't hesitate to adjudicate.
Soon the roads went back to being roads.
And all this while I hadn't noticed that borders
of two separate realms—
one visible, one erased; of khaki, of cashmere—
had threatened to weld along with two globes of fist.
The day I was finally told, I sat on the passenger seat of a fast car.
Father sat behind the wheel,
and Mandal's ghost was stationed right behind,
making funny faces at a naked boy peeing on the city council's wall;
chuckling out loud like he had when some biker
had dented our bumper, then cussed him out;
and doing some other strange unnameable thing as ghosts often do.
Father's flat palm was blindly outstretched toward me,
long enough that I thought he might be a tireless statue.
His face, blank and fixated on the distant red light.
My eyes and ears flew out to the world— mangled in unforgiving blur.
And it took more than pedigree and blood to place my palm onto his.

First published in *Mekong Review*, Issue 21, Nov 2020-Jan 2021

VISMAI RAO
**At the Kālachakra temple,
under a ceiling painted in bright oils,
I read eighteen kinds of emptiness**

I made one this morning: last spoon of honey
licked clean out of its jar—washed,

dried & recycled for storing loose tealeaf. Not yet noon,
I've already toured 23—Just yesterday,

we donated the dog-bed to the shelter & stood
in the newly vacated place, assessing size, weight,

how long in time will this one last?
Recyclable or not?—

The room inside my friend's lungs is mossed
with pneumonia, doctors restoring

the bit of empty
we all need to let the air in—Lao Tze

spoke of this: the use of the nothing
inside of things: the isn't in a water-can, a house,

the center of a wheel; the no-body
inside a body—

Last spring, beside the lake, among the reeds
we found a nest of broken egg shells—

what delight we took in this particular
kind of emptiness. Spent hours guessing what bird born

might have left it there—

First published in *trampset*, Dec 2020

Yamini Dand Shah
Salting the Earth

Act I | Scene 1

Tending to her gardens of salt,
navigating canals like Kanji Malam
with her *khampara*,
a proletarian toy of sifting
white from brown,
exegesis from excess:
a quarry of monotones.

Whitened in checkerboard pans,
Agariya's await a six-figure
compensation
for tastelessly
adding taste to Nation's
bl[ai:]ndness.

What can be flavour, grace and beauty,
can it not be a Rangoli?

Act I | Scene 2

Mud walls line her house.
cooks with muddy water

left for her by sand mafia.

Her meal of coarse rice and watery dal
is made on wood fire.
Treks for miles on parched earth,
dehydrated by Sun,
she swallows her spittle
{Water diviner ^ Sita}.

Metallic demons
replace muscle,

blankly,

offers a bowl of *chhaay*.

First published in *Abstract Oralism*, Paperwall Publishing, Sept 2021

YASHODHARA TRIVEDI
Empire of Hunger

I hate the Indians. They are a beastly people with a beastly
religion. The famine was their own fault for breeding like rabbits.
— Winston Churchill

They stole our harvest in steamers, love —
smiled tight at the ribs jutting out from our skin
like the wind rose on a pirate treasure map.
For twelve months we watched our city shrink
under stumbling feet as we tried to coax
kindness from men who lined their pockets with
our suffering. Babus in borrowed shoes and speech
siphoned every morsel to our name
to pay the piper of white greed.
I often wonder what secret Gods must
whisper to their wives as they
strain the foam from rice down our throats
in a belated peace offering. This high they stacked
our fallen friends down river banks we
raced around in better years on makeshift wheels.
You have to pinch your nose just right
or the stench can make you heave before
the fire in your hollow belly will. Most days
are a test to stay upright, but when the final plea
for a quiver of rain dwindles to dust at our blistered feet,
perhaps our spines will bow to greet
the stream of cherry blood kissing the street —
it is our only shot at making history.

First published in *Chestnut Review*, Winter 2021

ZAINAB UMMER FAROOK
Six Names for My Daughter

Iqra. In the beginning was the word and it was you, kanna.
An invitation to read, to delve into belief, to conjure dreams
from sparseness. Gold and orchard are beyond your mother
but you will always have reams of paper to parse: a story
to swim in, fat morsels of fable and myth, and if you wait,
a poem, so you can coax silences out of many a noisy box.

Someday, Ruhi, you will learn of Pandora and her infernal box.
Until then, may these worn touchstones serve you well, kanna:
look past the very last page of every tale. Once it turns, wait
for three beats. Wonder aloud why after folly, after fever-dream,
after freeing plague and peril, P held true to hope-spirit. Stories
ought to be sifted; let no one deter you, not even your mother.

I was told when I have a kid of my own, I'd know: smothering
is always a slip away. I leave a trail of clipped wings, boxes
I was ushered into, circles of chalk. Shikha, here is a storied
lineage of moms who hem in songbird and flame. But kanna,
mother-promise, I won't sing you into tyranny. If you dream
into life a wildfire, I'll pray for you to clear new ground. I'll wait

and watch you hopscotch across borders. You aren't born to wait.
Your feet obey no maps and leap over wire-fences, this mother
of yours in tow, giggling. You finger-paint swatches of dream-
fabric, refuse to call them flags. Ashima, my pulpit is a soapbox.

But you house tomorrow's sermons in your artless body, kanna.
Your paper-boats romp through high seas, sans pomp, sans story.

Braiding smoke and starlight with ease, you take to telling stories
as tadpole to swamp-water, dappled green. There is no waiting
for you anymore, words windswept, curls unkempt. Kanna,
my mole-kissing, tale-spinning Zia, how is it that you mother
metaphor and simile, multiverse cradled in your mouth, unboxing
all feeling, outfoxing all my attempts to hasbi-rabbi you into dreams?

You send oxblood talismans from sandcastles yet to be dreamt,
warding off home-breakers. Will your name ripple in lore, history?
Or will it be a memory they trip over when tinny music-boxes
sing of it in back-alleys? Claws naked, this country once waited
and witnessed you coming to roost, the falcon that mothered
rage and rebellion. Shaheen: soaring wing, talon, beak, my kanna—

but listen, wait! I have yearned for you since the day my mother
locked up all my storybooks (*I will be a better mom than you,
nokkikko!*) but kanna, you're a dream I float downriver in a box

First published in *Nether Quarterly*, March 2021

ZEENAT KHAN

–Time–

i s———w a s———w·i l l

a fugitive	sky encircling	a w o m b
o n i o n	peeling an' weeping	salt - tears
s n a k e	s p i r a l l i n g d o w n	the breathing
w a v e s	rising falling departing to	return back to
a s e a	ready to s w a l l o w you	inside blue green
f l a m e	f l i c k e r i n g in f e a r of	g u s t - h a n d s
a dream-	fallin' cataracts on eyes	from the sky
pilgrim	wandering searching	unnamed tomb
a worm	inside peas cocoon & knees	of s k e l e t a l s
p a w s	disappearing and appearing	in dense forest
islands	napping like twinkling stars	in wet nest
blo od	flowing i n s i d e veins	mountains
may be	a boiled word and	everything
made-up	ochre urns of	d u s t

as i—you——we
when
time seems nothing and everything

First published in *Hakara Journal*, Edition 14: Dust, June 2021

ZILKA JOSEPH
Sailor, Do Not Go
for my father, Sunny (Solomon)

You did not go gently into the night
cursed old age and refused to back away
raged against the rising sea, dying light

Solomon your wisdom crushed in this plight
face muzzled by mask, tongue shrunk in the fray
How could you go gently into that night

Brave warrior, you scorned the last wave's height
yet denied how frail our deeds, our flesh's way
raged against us, our pleas, the dimming light

Wild sailor you were, drunk with your own might
who found at last our bodies are just clay
no, you did not go gently into night

Sunny, even dying, your name is filled with light
your blind eyes cried, shot eagle as you lay
wingless, you raged, still unvanquished by night

My father now your voyage-end in sight
helpless, our hands cling, I beg— go, no stay
we *will not* go gentle into night
rage against separation, the dark light

(*after Dylan Thomas*)

First published in *Big Scream 60*, 2021

249

THE EDITORS' CONTRIBUTIONS

Sukrita Paul Kumar, former Fellow of Indian Institute of Advanced Study, Shimla, held the prestigious Aruna Asaf Ali Chair at Delhi University. An honorary faculty at Corfu, Greece, she was an invited resident poet at the prestigious International Writing Programme at Iowa, USA. Her most recent collections of poems are *Vanishing Words*, *Country Drive* and *Dream Catcher*. Her critical books include *Narrating Partition*, *The New Story and Conversations on Modernism*. She has co-edited many books, including *Speaking for Herself: Asian Women's Writings*. An Honorary Fellow at HK Baptist University, Hong Kong, she has published many translations and has held exhibitions of her paintings.

SUKRITA
Dialogues with Ganga

The emerald green of the river-waters is
the green of the forests softened
The blue is that of the skies
And the brown
that of the mud
Carried to the plains

With many a million corpses and ashes
In your belly
What of the colour of death
O Ganga?

But death you confirm has no colour
It is transparent like truth

*

In the din of the river
The sound of the universe vanishes
And echoes of silence rise
From within the mind
As confessions

O Ganga,
I am ready to
Perform my life again

*

When there is lightening
Falling on your chest
From the coal-ash skies above
Why do you not pause,
Hold on to it tight
O Ganga

For the forests to light up
For the hanging bats and owls
to go back into dark holes

Let the birds fly and chirp
Let the nightmares crumble
Into daylight and cheer

Shed all ghosts and demons
To the oblivion
Fill the void with music
Of your fast-moving waters

*

In Sanskrit, Ganga is called
Trilokapatha-gamini
One who travels thousands of miles
Across three worlds

O Ganga,
Here when I meet you this instant
I wake up to your energy
Vibrating in the unrelenting flow
All three worlds coming together
Here and now

First published in *Confluence*, UK, May 2021

Author of four books of poetry — *Two Full Moons* (Bombaykala Books*)*, *Words Not Spoken*, *The Longest Pleasure* and *The Silk of Hunger*, Vinita Agrawal is an award-winning poet, editor and translator. She is based in Indore. She is the joint recipient of the Rabindranath Tagore Literary Prize 2018 and winner of the Gayatri GaMarsh Memorial Award for Literary Excellence, USA, 2015. She is Poetry Editor with *Usawa Literary Review*. She edited an anthology on climate change titled *Open Your Eyes* in 2020. She edited a Memoir-Anthology on the Kashmiri poet Ghulam Rasool Nazki in 2021. Most recently, Vinita co-edited the *Yearbook of Indian Poetry in English* 2020-21. She is on the Advisory Board of the Tagore Literary Prize and on the Global Judging Panel of the SheInsprawrds. She is deeply connected to animals and nature. Read more about her at www.vinitawords.com.

VINITA AGRAWAL
Splendid Poison Frog

Was it a cold December Wednesday
when you left?
A frosty, flinty, pin-point moment
that seals most pull-outs.
Silent like a hushed Mayday signal
reverberating in the ripples of a pond.
What time exactly
did you hop over
to where nowhere exists?
Did the sun flicker
at your vanishing act?
The way yellow convulses on a color palette
when mixed with green
before turning blue.
Was it the hour of dusk,
your favorite hour,
when you looked your dashing, heart-throb best
skin, brilliant coral, eyes, kohl black.
A fungus with a long name
colonized your body.
A local phenomena, some said.
Like a cloud breaking-up
a balmy summer's evening.
Did the next morning feel
like a fine after-showers morning?

Estimated Extinction date: 2020
Cause: Chytrid Fungus (Batrachochytrium dendrobatidis)

First published in *Mascara Literary Review* Issue 27, December 2021

BEACON LIGHTS

ADIL JUSSAWALLA
Like Dictators

Rats are strict in their regulations.
Like dictators they regulate
meals and nations
along lines of bite.

First published in *The Tattooed Teetotaller and other wonders* (August 2021, Poetrywala).

Adil Jussawalla was born in Bombay in 1940. *The Tattooed Teetotaller* is his sixth book of poems. His third, *Trying to Say Goodbye*, published in 2011, was honoured with a Sahitya Akademi award in 2014. He lives in Bombay.

Keki N. Daruwalla
Extract From Sappho Poems

Goddess I am lonely now,
a tragic harvest in your net,
the Pleiades and the moon have set,
I sleep alone.

Love's delirium does not last;
I've learnt that lesson from the past,
the emptiness that follows lust
scars me to the bone.

Love's desertions, they are swift,
as star-clusters incline and shift.
My lovers like Orion drift,
I drift alone.

First published in *Poetry at Sangam*, July 2021

Keki N. Daruwalla is one of India's foremost poets and writers. His ten volumes of poetry include *Under Orion, The Keeper of the Dead* (winner of the Sahitya Akademi Award, 1984), *Landscapes* (winner of the Commonwealth Poetry Award, Asia, 1987), *Night River and The Map-maker*. His first novel, *For Pepper* and *Christ*, was shortlisted for the Commonwealth Fiction Prize in 2010. He was awarded the Padma Shri in 2014. Most recently, he was honoured with the Poet Laureate award at the Tata Literature Live! Mumbai Litfest, 2017. His work has been translated into Spanish, Swedish, Magyar, German and Russian.

JAYANTA MAHAPATRA
After the Death of a Friend

Over, the kite's flight; and of a sudden
is the realisation of the morning overcome
by the echo of dark nights, silent witness
to the colourlessness crouching down before us.
Stealing time is what's been happening all the time.
Is it because you've heard only your own cries,
fifty years earlier too, as they go by, adulterated with death?
Or some shy crumpled laughter carrying with it
the air of an unspoken but certain defeat?
Somewhere in my mind, I lose the ability
to disappear, as the morning air moves listlessly about,
indifferent to looks or history or roots. And here,
if I died, like this, dying for the person I was,
or for the one I see coming in and out of your death,
would that be a way out to save me
from the solitude I've believed in and pursued
in the same way I pursue the rush of blood in my veins?

There is so much we've begun to pile up on you, more
than all the lives we've had and have lost. Nothing whatever

burns to ash. Years pass. Days, wisdom, the simple sadness.
A slow, moving Ray of sunlight walks me backwards
to a past turned magical by virtue of its emptiness,
this part of myself that never fails to embrace us.

First published in *The Paris Review*, Winter 2020

Jayanta Mahapatra was born on 22 October 1928 (age 94 years), in Cuttack. He is the author of twenty seven books of poetry. He is the first Indian poet to win a Sahitya Akademi award for English poetry. He is the author of poems such as 'Indian Summer' and 'Hunger', which are regarded as classics in modern Indian English literature. Most recently, he has published his autobiography in Oriya.

ABOUT THE POETS

Abhay K. is the author of nine poetry collections and the editor of *The Book of Bihari Literature* (HarperCollins, 2022), *The Bloomsbury Anthology of Great Indian Poems, CAPITALS, New Brazilian Poems* and *The Bloomsbury Book of Great Indian Love Poems.* His poems have appeared in over 100 literary magazines including *Poetry Salzburg Review, Asia Literary Review* among others.

Abhishek Anicca is a writer, poet and performer. He identifies as a person with locomotor disability and chronic illness which shapes his creative endeavours. His poems have been published in *nether Quarterly, Gulmohur Quarterly, Indian Cultural Forum, The Sunflower Collective, The Alipore Post* and others.

Achita Khare, while born and brought up in Datia, MP, believes she truly grew up in Bangalore. She tries to make sense of numbers by the day (a marketer by profession) and words at night. Her poems have been featured in *The Gulmohur Quarterly* and *Verses of Silence.*

Adithya Patil is pursuing his Bachelor's in Economics, and lives in Bangalore. His work appears in different publications including *The Drabble, Scarlett Leaf Review, Literary Yard, Borderless Journal, Eskimo Pie, Muse India, Modern Literature, Litehouse, Spillwords, EKL Review* and elsewhere.

Aditya Shankar's poetry and translations are in reputed journals and anthologies around the world. He has been nominated for Best of the Net and Pushcart Prize multiple times. His book *XXL* was shortlisted for the Yuva Puraskar (Sahitya Akademi). *After Seeing* and *Party Poopers* are his other books.

Aekta Khubchandani is matriculating her dual MFA in Creative Writing (Poetry & Nonfiction) from The New School in NY. Her fiction, *Love in Bengali Dialect*, is nominated for Best American Short Fiction anthology. Her essay, "Holes in the Body," published by *Entropy*, is featured on Lit Hub's Best of Weekly Literary.

Afsar Mohammad teaches at the University of Pennsylvania, and he has published five volumes of poetry in Telugu and his English poetry will be out soon. He has also published a monograph with the Oxford University Press with a title *The Festival of Pirs: Popular Islam and Shared Devotion in South India*.

Ajay Kumar lives in Chennai, India, where he's pursuing his BA in English Language and Literature. His works have appeared in *The Bombay Literary Magazine*, *Rattle*, *The Bombay Review*, *Muse India*, among others.

Amit Shankar Saha is the author of three collections of poems titled *Balconies of Time*, *Fugitive Words*, and *Illicit Poems*. A Pushcart Prize, Griffin Poetry Prize, and Best of Net nominee, he has a PhD in English from Calcutta University and teaches at Seacom Skills University. His website is www.amitshankarsaha.com.

Amlanjyoti Goswami's new book *Vital Signs* (Poetrywala) follows his earlier collection *River Wedding* (Poetrywala). His poetry has been published in notable journals and anthologies around the world. A Best of the Net and Pushcart nominee, he grew up in Guwahati and lives in Delhi.

Anannya Uberoi was born in Delhi, and now lives in Madrid. She is poetry editor at *The Bookends Review*, the winner of the

6th Singapore Poetry Contest and a Pushcart Prize nominee. Her work has appeared in *The Birmingham Arts Journal, The Emerson Review,* and *Poetry Salzburg Review.* www. anannyauberoi.com

Anjali Purohit is a painter, writer, poet, translator and curator. She is the author of two books, *Ragi Ragini: Chronicles from Aji's Kitchen* (Yoda Press, 2012) and *Go Talk to the River: the Ovis of Bahinabai Choudhari* (Yoda Press, 2019). She is the founder and curator of The Cappuccino Adda (formerly, Cappuccino Readings), an initiative to foster a literary café culture in Mumbai. She can be found at anjaliwrites.com

Ankur is from India. Some of his published poems and stories can be found in, among others, *Cha: An Asian Literary Journal, Mascara Literary Review, Voice & Verse Poetry Magazine,* and *Rattle.* His first full collection of poems, titled *The Four Colors,* was published in July 2020 (Hawakal Publishers).

Ankush Banerjee is a poet, mental health professional and Naval officer, based in New Delhi. Author of *An Essence of Eternity* (Sahitya Akademi, 2016), his work has appeared in *Indian Literature, Eclectica, Cha, Aainanagar* and elsewhere. He is pursuing his PhD in Masculinity Studies from BITS, Pilani.

Anna Lynn is a research scholar at EFL University. Her areas of interest include women's writing, art and cinema. The anxieties of a feminine heart are a constant muse and as the Woolfian stream passes, she presses watered images into writing. Her work can be found on *Sunflower Collective, The Chakkar, Gulmohur Quarterly, In Plainspeak,* and her blog www.seagirlstories.wordpress.com.

Antara Mukherjee has a Masters in English Literature and has worked as a communication professional. Her work has appeared in *Kitaab, Sahitya Akademi, Muse India, The Chakkar, Teesta Review, Verse of Silence*. Her short story won the 'All India Literature Competition,' — Anthelion School of Arts. She has co-written a playscript which is under production in Bangalore.

Aranya is a poet, and editor of the digital newsletter, *Poetly*. He is currently based out of Delhi, a place to which he does not belong.

Arun Paria lives in Pune; writes poetry, fiction and creative non-fiction. His poems have been published in *The Bombay Literary Magazine, nether Quarterly*; and his fiction in *EKL Review*, creative non-fiction in *White Wall Review*, Toronto. He is the founder of Pune Writers' Group, a community serving over 2000 writers.

Ashwani Kumar is a poet, political scientist and professor at Tata Institute of Social Sciences, Mumbai.

Aswin Vijayan is an Assistant Professor at the Zamorin's Guruvayurappan College, Calicut and has an MA in Poetry from the Seamus Heaney Centre, Queen's University Belfast. His poems have been published in *Witness: The Red River Book of Poetry of Dissent, The Bombay Literary Magazine*, and *The Tangerine* among others.

Avinab Datta-Areng is the author of *Annus Horribilis*. He's also the editor of *nether* and currently lives in Goa.

Babitha Marina Justin is an academic, a poet and an artist. Her works have appeared in *Taylor and Francis Journals, Marshal Cavendish*, the *Yearbook* (2020), *Singing in the Dark, Eclectica, Esthetic Apostle, Jaggery*, etc. Her books are *Of Fireflies, Guns and the Hills* (Poetry, 2015), *I Cook My Own Feast* (Poetry, 2019), *salt, pepper and silverlinings: celebrating our grandmothers* (2019).

Basudhara Roy teaches English at Karim City College affiliated to Kolhan University, Chaibasa. She is the author of two collections of poems, *Moon in my Teacup* (Kolkata: Writer's Workshop, 2019) and *Stitching a Home* (New Delhi: Red River, 2021). She loves, rebels, writes and reviews from Jamshedpur, Jharkhand, India.

Bharti Bansal is a poet from Shimla, Himachal Pradesh. Poetry is her way of self-healing. Her works have been published in magazines like *Aaduna, Harness Magazine, Oc87recoverydiaries.org, The Vocal and The Prologue Magazine* of the Hindu college, DU. Her works have appeared in books like *Heavy lies the Crown, Love as we Know it* and *Sunflowers on the Horizon*.

Bhaswati Ghosh writes and translates fiction, non-fiction and poetry. Her first book of fiction is *Victory Colony, 1950*. Her first work of translation from Bengali into English, *My Days with Ramkinkar Baij*, won her the Charles Wallace (India) Trust Fellowship for translation. Bhaswati's writing has appeared in several literary journals.

Debarshi Mitra's second book *Osmosis* was published by Hawakal in 2020. His works have previously appeared in anthologies like *Yearbook of Indian Poetry* and *Best Indian Poetry 2018* and in journals like *The Shore, Guftugu, The Pangolin Review, Coldnoon, Indiana Voice Journal, The Indian Cultural Forum*, among various others.

Debasis Tripathy was born in Odisha, India. His poems have appeared or are forthcoming in *Decomp, UCity Review, Rogue Agent, Leon Lit, Vayavya, Mantle Poetry*, and several other journals online and in print. He lives in Bangalore.

Devanshi Khetarpal is the editor-in-chief of *Inklette Magazine*. Her work has been published in *Poetry at Sangam, The Bombay Literary Magazine, nether*, and *Vayavya*, among others. Her poetry collection, *Small Talk* was published by Writers Workshop in 2019. She is from Bhopal, India, and lives in New York City.

A monochromatic leaves enthusiast, Divyanshi Dash believes in poetry as a prayer. Her work has appeared in *The Walled City Journal, Ayaskala*, and *Stone of Madness Press* among others. Even though she is currently based in New Delhi, India, she lives between crying and dancing.

Durga Prasad Panda is an accomplished bilingual poet and critic whose poems have been included in significant anthologies like *Yearbook of Indian Poetry in English 2020-21, Shape of a Poem: Red River Book of Contemporary Erotic Poetry, Witness: A Red River Anthology of Dissent*. He edited *A Reader on Jayanta Mahapatra* for Sahitya Akademi.

Hailing from the beautiful state of Kerala, Feby Joseph describes himself as a spiritual vagabond. He's working as a Piano teacher in Mumbai. He is the winner of Reuel International Prize, Poetry, 2020. Some of his works have appeared on *Café Dissensus*, *Foreign Literary Journal* and *The Bangalore Review*.

Gayatri Lakhiani Chawla is an award-winning poet, translator and French teacher from Mumbai. She is the author of two poetry collections, *Invisible Eye* and *The Empress*. Her poem won a special mention award by Architectural Journalism and Criticism 2020.

Gayatri Majumdar is editor, publisher and founder of critically acclaimed Indian literary journal, *The Brown Critique*. While Brown Critique Books has been publishing several books over the past couple of decades, Gayatri began her career as a journalist in Press Trust of India and The Independent (India) in Mumbai. She was assistant editor of The Indian P.E.N. Her career also encompasses leadership in the publishing industry.

Geetha Ravichandran is a bureaucrat from Chennai. Her poems have been published in several online journals including *Borderless*, *The Literary Nest*, *Madras Courier*, *The Pangolin Review*. Her poems have been included in a couple of anthologies published by Hawakal — *Hibiscus* and *Shimmer Spring*.

Gopal Lahiri is a bilingual poet, critic, editor, writer and translator with 23 books published, including five jointly edited books. His poetry is also published across various anthologies as well as in eminent journals of India and abroad. His poems are translated in 16 languages.

Gopikrishnan Kottoor won the All-India Poetry Competitions in both the General and Social Jury categories. His latest poetry collection *Swan Lake* has just been released. He edits the online poetry journal www.chipmunk.co.in

Gopika Jadeja is a bi-lingual poet and translator from

India, writing in English and Gujarati. Gopika is working on a literary project that deals with archival materials—de-centering and challenging colonial epistemologies.

Huzaifa Pandit works as an Assistant Professor, English in Department of Higher Education, Jammu and Kashmir. His maiden book *Green is the Colour of Memory* won the won the first edition of Rhythm Divine Poets Chapbook Contest 2017. Besides he has won several poetry contests, including Glass House Poetry Competition and Bound Poetry Contest.

Indu Parvathi is a teacher and poet from Bengaluru, India. Her work has been published in various literary magazines and journals including *The Sunflower Collective, Punch Magazine, nether Quarterly* and *The Alipore Post*. Her first volume of poetry, *On the Sidewalk*, was published by Authorspress, India in 2019.

Ishmeet Kaur Chaudhry (educationist, author, poet) teaches at Central University of Gujarat, Gandhinagar. She was recognised as an Inspired Teacher for The President of India's In-residence Program in June 2015. She is associated with The Guru Granth Sahib Project (Translation and Transcreation of selected compositions), an initiative of SikhRI, USA.

Jagari Mukherjee, winner of the Reuel International Prize for Poetry 2019, is a poet, editor, and reviewer based in Kolkata. Jagari has authored three collections of poetry—a chapbook and two full-length volumes. She won the Women Empowered Gifted Poet Award in 2021, among other prizes.

Jhilam Chattaraj is an academic and poet based in Hyderabad, India. *Noise Cancellation* (Hawakal Publishers) is her latest collection of poetry.

Jinendra Jain is studying MA in Creative Writing at Lasalle College of Arts Singapore, a degree conferred by Goldsmiths, University of London. A retired banker, he has worked in various trading and risk management roles for twenty-five years, after graduating from the Indian Institute of Technology Kanpur and the Indian Institute of Management Calcutta.

Jonaki Ray worked as a software engineer (briefly), and is now a poet, writer, and editor. Her work has appeared in *POETRY, Poetry Wales, The Rumpus, Indian Literature*, and elsewhere. Her poetry collection, *Firefly Memories*, is forthcoming from Copper Coin in 2022.

Jyotirmoy Sil is a dilettante poet who writes in English and Bengali. Presently he is an Assistant Professor of English in Malda College, West Bengal. His poems have been published in *Muse India, Madras Courier, Spillwords, International Times, Bichitrapatra, Aparjan*, and *Achin pakhi*.

K Srilata was a writer in residence at the University of Stirling, Scotland and Sangam house. Her latest collection of poems, *The Unmistakable Presence of Absent Humans*, was published by Poetrywala in 2019. Other books: *The Rapids of a Great River: The Penguin Book of Tamil Poetry* and *All the Worlds Between: A Collaborative Poetry Project Between India and Ireland*.

Kandala Singh lives in New Delhi, in a flat that looks out at Ashoka trees, and escapes to the mountains as often as she can. Her poems have appeared in *Rattle*, *SWWIM Every Day*, *Hindustan Times* and *The Alipore Post*, among other places.

Karan Kapoor is a poet based in New Delhi with an MA in Literary Art Creative Writing from Ambedkar University. A recent winner of the Red Wheelbarrow Prize judged by Mark Doty, his poems have appeared or are forthcoming in *Plume*, *Rattle*, *The Indian Quarterly*, *The Bombay Literary Magazine* and elsewhere.

Kartikay is a 27-year-old bilingual poet from Kanpur by birth and Mumbai by heart, who forever finds his voice traversing between English and Hindustani. His original work has featured in *Narrow Road Journal*, *The Alipore Post*, *deCenter Magazine*, *Gulmohar Quarterly*, and *Jaggery*; and a translation in *The Usawa Literary Review*.

Kashiana Singh calls herself a work practitioner and embodies the essence of her TEDx talk — Work as Worship into her everyday. She proudly serves as Managing Editor for Poets Reading the News. Her newest collection *Woman by the Door* is coming up in 2022 with Apprentice House Press.

Kavita Ezekiel Mendonca was born and raised in a Jewish family in Mumbai. Her first book of poems, *Family Sunday and other Poems*, was published in 1989. Her poem 'How to light up a Poem' was nominated for a Pushcart Prize. *Light of the Sabbath* is her recently published chapbook.

Kinjal Sethia is an independent writer and editor. Her work has been published in *nether Quarterly*, *Borderless* and *Samyukta Fiction*. She is the Fiction Editor at *The Bombay Literary Magazine* and the Books Editor at *Usawa Literary Review*. She is a part of collectives The Quarantine Train and Pune Writers' Group.

Kinshuk Gupta is a medical student and a poet. He was longlisted for the People Need Change Poetry Contest (2020), The Poetry Society, UK; Awards for Creative Writing (2021) and shortlisted for Srinivas Rayparol Poetry Prize (2021). He edits poetry for *Jaggery Lit* and *Mithila Review* and works as an associate editor for the *Usawa Literary Review*.

Kiran Bhat is an Indian-American author. He is known as the author of *we of the forsaken world...* He has published books in five different languages, and got his writing published in journals such as *The Kenyon Review*, *The Chakkar*, and many other places.

Kiriti Sengupta, the 2018 Rabindranath Tagore Literary Prize recipient, is a poet, editor, translator, and publisher. He has authored eleven books of poetry and prose; two books of translation and edited eight anthologies. He is the founder and chief editor of the *Ethos Literary Journal*. Sengupta lives in New Delhi.

Kuhu Joshi is a poet from New Delhi, currently an MFA candidate at Sarah Lawrence College. She was nominated for Best New Poets 2021. Her work appears in *Rattle, petrichor, Sonic Boom,* and *The Bombay Literary Magazine,* among others. She is the author of the photo-chapbook *Private Maps.*

Kunjana Parashar is a poet from Mumbai. Her poems have been published in *Poetry Northwest, The Indian Quarterly, SWWIM Every Day, UCity Review, The Bombay Literary Magazine,* and elsewhere. She is the recipient of the Toto Funds the Arts award for poetry & the Deepankar Khiwani Memorial Prize.

Kushal Poddar, an author and a father, edited a magazine, *Words Surfacing,* authored seven volumes, including *The Circus Came To My Island, A Place For Your Ghost Animals, Eternity Restoration Project: selected and new poems* and *Herding My Thoughts To The Slaughterhouse—A Prequel.* His works have been translated into ten languages.

Lakshmi Kannan has published twenty-seven books till date that include poems, novels, short stories and translations in English. Her recent publications are *Wooden Cow* (Translation), 2021), *Sipping the Jasmine Moon*, Poems (2019) and *The Glass Bead Curtain*, Novel (2020 c2016). Please visit www.lakshmikannan.in

Lina Krishnan is based in Auroville. She has participated in poetry festivals across India, and her poems, nonfiction writing, abstract art and photographs have found a place in literary journals, arts magazines, exhibitions and in six anthologies of poetry. Lina is addicted to outmoded cinema, among other things.

Maaz Bin Bilal is a poet, translator, and academic. His first book of poems, *Ghazalnama: Poems from Delhi, Belfast, and Urdu* (2019) was shortlisted for the Sahitya Akademi Yuva Puraskar. Maaz was the Charles Wallace Fellow in writing and translation at Wales in 2018-19 and holds a PhD from Queen's University Belfast. He is associate professor of literary studies at Jindal Global University.

Malachi Edwin Vethamani is a Malaysian Indian writer and emeritus professor. His publications include *Complicated Lives* (2016), *Life Happens* (2017), *Coitus Interruptus and Other Stories* (2018), *Malchin Testament: Malaysian Poems* (2018), *Ronggeng-Ronggeng: Malaysian Short Stories* (2020) and *Malaysian Millennial Voices* (2021). He is Founding Editor of *Men Matters Online Journal*.

Mani Rao is the author of fifteen books/chapbooks, primarily in poetry. Her latest works include *Sing to Me* (Recent Works) and *Living Mantra: Mantra, Deity and Visionary Experience Today* (Palgrave Macmillan). Rao has held fellowships and residencies at Iowa IWP, Omi Ledig House and IPSI Canberra.

Manik Sharma is a journalist and a culture writer who writes for leading newspapers and journals. He is a consulting editor at *Arré*. He has two books of poetry to his credit and his poems have featured in various journals. He has co-edited a poetry anthology, *A Map Called Home*, published by Kitaab, Singapore (2018).

Manisha Sharma is a poet and fiction writer. Her work is published or is forthcoming in *Arts & Letters, The Fourth River, Madison Review, Puerto Del Sol, The Bombay Review* and more. She earned an MFA in creative writing from Virginia Tech. Details about Manisha are at www.manisha-sharma.com.

Meenakshi Mohan, an internationally published writer, is an educator, art critic, children's writer, painter, and poet. She has been listed twice in the Who is Who Among American Teachers. She is on the editorial Committee for *Inquiry in Education*, a peer-reviewed journal published by National Louis University, Chicago, Illinois.

Michelle D'costa is the author of the poetry chapbook *Gulf* (Yavanika Press, 2021). She is the co-host of the author interview podcast, "Books and Beyond With Bound." Her poetry was longlisted for the TOTO Award For Creative Writing 2021. Her fiction and poetry can be found in various journals online.

Minal Sarosh has done her Masters in English Literature from Gujarat University. She has published two poetry collections *Mitosis & Other Poems* (1992) and *A Lizard's Tail and Other Poems* (2020). Her two novels are *Soil for My Roots* (2015) and *Wicked Money* (2020). She lives in Ahmedabad.

Moumita Alam is a poet and teacher. Her poems have been published by *Freedom Review, The Bibliophilia Café*, etc. Her book *The Musings of the Dark* has been published recently and is available in Amazon. She is also a contributory writer to *The People's Review*.

Mrinalini Harchandrai is the author of *A Bombay in My Beat*, a collection of poetry. Her short fiction has been longlisted for the Commonwealth Short Story Prize 2018 and shortlisted for *Columbia Journal* Spring 2020 Contest. She is Deputy Editor at *Poetry at Sangam*.

Mustansir Dalvi is an anglophone poet, translator and editor. His two books of poems in English are *Brouhahas of Cocks* (Poetrywala, 2013) and *Cosmopolitician* (Poetrywala, 2018). Mustansir Dalvi teaches architecture in Mumbai.

Nabanita Sengupta, translator and creative writer, is an Assistant Professor of English in Kolkata. She has authored *The Ghumi Days* (Juggernaut), translated *A Bengali Lady in England* (Shambhabi Imprint), and *Chambal Revisited* (Hawakal), co-edited the first IPPL anthology of poems, *Voices and Vision* (Virasat) and a volume of critical essays, *Understanding Women's Displacement* (Routledge).

Nabina Das is a poet and writer based in Hyderabad. She is the author of *Sanskarnama, Into the Migrant City*, and *Blue Vessel*. Her forthcoming volume, *Anima and the Narrative Limits*, will be published by Yoda Press this year. Her first book of translations *Arise Out of the Lock: 50 Bangladeshi Women Poets* to commemorate the golden jubilee of Bangladesh is coming soon from Balestier Press, UK. She has also published a short fiction collection and a novel.

Namratha Varadharajan writes to explore emotions, relationships and our interconnectedness with nature and tries to chip at the prejudices that plague us, one syllable at a time. She is the co-founder of Soul Craft Poetry Workshops. Her poetry and short stories have been widely anthologized. She writes at http://namysaysso.com.

Nandini Sahu, Professor of English and Director, School of Foreign Languages, IGNOU, New Delhi, India, is an established Indian English poet. An author/editor of fifteen books, she is the recipient of Gold Medal from the Hon'ble Vice President of India for her contributions to English Studies.

Neeti Singh is a poet, translator and Associate Professor of English. She writes and researches in areas of Bhakti and Cultural Studies, and teaches in the Department of English, Faculty of Arts, The Maharaja Sayajirao University of Baroda, Gujarat. She has published over twenty-five research papers and five books till date.

Neha R. Krishna is a poet from Mumbai. Her work has been published in *Under the Basho, Presence, Frogpond, Haiku Masters, Chrysanthemum, Failed Haiku, Human/Kind Journal, Frameless Sky, Haiku Foundation, Bones, Prune Juice, Moonbathing, Wild Plum, Asahi Haiku Network.*

Nikita Parik holds a Master's in Linguistics, a three-year diploma in French, and another Master's in English. *Diacritics of Desire* (2019) is her debut book of poems, followed by *Amour and Apocalypse* (2020), a novel in translation. She currently edits *EKL Review.*

Nishi Pulugurtha is an academic and creative writer based in Kolkata. Her publications include *Derozio* (2010), *Out in the Open* (2019), *Across and Beyond* (2020), *The Real and the Unreal and Other Poems* (2020), *The Window Sill* (fiction, 2021) and a second volume of poems is forthcoming.

Pervin Saket was awarded the Srinivas Rayaprol Poetry Prize 2021 and received the inaugural Fellowship for the Vancouver Manuscript Intensive (2021). Pervin is Poetry Editor of *The Bombay Literary Magazine*, co-founder of the Dum Pukht Writers' Workshop and Managing Editor at The Quarantine Train: A Writers' Collective.

Preeti Parikh is an Indian American writer living in Ohio. With a past educational background in medicine and a recent MFA from The Rainier Writing Workshop, she is currently working on a book-length poetry collection. Preeti's poems and essays appear in *Nonwhite and Woman*, *Kweli Journal*, *Literary Mama*, and elsewhere.

Preeti Vangani is the author of *Mother Tongue Apologize* (RLFPA Editions, 2019). Her work has appeared in *Threepenny Review*, *Gulf Coast*, *Hobart*, among other journals, and has been supported by Ucross, Djerassi and California Center for Innovation. She currently teaches at the University of San Francisco.

Priya Sarukkai Chabria is an award-winning poet, translator and writer of nine books and editor of two anthologies. Her books include *Andal The Autobiography of a Goddess* (translation), *Sing of Life Revisioning Tagore's Gitanjali* (poetry), *Clone* (speculative fiction) and *Bombay/Mumbai: Immersions* (non-fiction). www.priyasarukkaichabria.com

Purabi Bhattacharya is a writer, poet, involved in teaching and writing for over a decade now. She is the author of two collections of poems, *Sand Column* (2019) and *Call Me* (2015), both published by Writers Workshop, India; and reviews books for *Muse India*.

Ra Sh has published four collections of poetry: *Architecture of Flesh, The Bullet Train and other loaded poems, Kintsugi by Hadni* and a chapbook, *In the Mirror, our graves* and a play, *Blind Men Write.* His poems have been translated to Italian, German, French, Spanish, Danish and Indonesian.

Rahana K Ismail is a poet and a doctor from Calicut, Kerala. Her work has appeared in *nether Quarterly, Verse of Silence* and *EKL Review.* She can be reached at rahanakismail@gmail. com when she is done rummaging through the woodsorrel, ironweeds and adiantum with her daughter.

Rajiv Mohabir is the author of three collections of poetry including *Cutlish* (Four Way Books 2021) which was awarded the Eric Hoffer Medal Provacateur, longlisted for the 2022 PEN/Voelcker Prize, and was a finalist for the National Book Critics Books Award. He teaches in the MFA program at Emerson College and lives in the Boston area.

Ranjit Hoskote's books include *Vanishing Acts* (Penguin, 2006), *Central Time* (Penguin, 2014), *Jonahwhale* (Penguin, 2018; in the UK as *The Atlas of Lost Beliefs*, Arc, 2020) and *Hunchprose* (Penguin, 2021). Hoskote's translation of a 14th-century Kashmiri woman mystic has appeared as *I, Lalla: The Poems of Lal Ded* (Penguin, 2011).

Ranu Uniyal is a bilingual poet from Lucknow. She is Professor and Head Department of English, University of Lucknow. She has written four books of poetry: *Across the Divide* (2006), *December Poems* (2012), *The Day We Went Strawberry Picking In Scarborough* (2018) and *Saeeda Ke Ghar*

(Hindi poems, 2021). She also works for people with special needs in Lucknow (PYSSUM.org).

Rishi Dastidar's second collection of poetry, *Saffron Jack*, is published in the UK by Nine Arches Press. He is also editor of *The Craft: A Guide to Making Poetry Happen in the 21st Century* (Nine Arches Press), and co-editor of *Too Young, Too Loud, Too Different: Poems from Malika's Poetry Kitchen* (Corsair).

Fictionist | Poet | Critic | Screenwriter | Poetry-workshop Conductor, Rochelle Potkar is the author of *Four Degrees of Separation, Paper Asylum, Bombay Hangovers*, and the co-author of *The Coordinates of Us/*सर्व अंशांतून आपण. @ rochellepotkar, She blogs at: https://rochellepotkar.com/

Rohan Chhetri's latest book is *Lost, Hurt, or in Transit Beautiful* (Winner of the Kundiman Poetry Prize), published in India by HarperCollins. His poems have appeared in *The Paris Review*, Academy of American Poets' *Poem-a-Day, Revue Europe*, among others.

Rohini Kejriwal is a writer, poet and a curator based out of Bangalore. She is always up for a good story, travel, strong coffee and the company of plants. She runs *The Alipore Post*, a curated newsletter and journal to promote contemporary art, poetry, photography, music and all things intriguing.

Ronald Tuhin D'Rozario works have been published on *Café Dissensus Everyday, Narrow Road Literary Journal, Kitaab, The Pangolin Review, The Alipore Post, Grey Sparrow Press, The Chakkar, Plato's Caves Online, RIC Journal, The Walled City Journal, Beyond the Panorama, Verse of Silence* and other places.

Roopam Mishra is a Research Scholar at the Department of English, and Modern European Languages, University of Lucknow. Her works have appeared or are forthcoming in *Confluence Magazine*, *Setu*, *Rusty Truck*, *Café Dissensus*, *Borderless Journal*, *Hastaksher*, etc.

Sagari Chhabra is an award-winning author and filmmaker. Her books include *The Professional Women's Dreams*, *The Talking Tree* and *In Search of Freedom* which was awarded the National Laadli Media award. Her films have won five national and international awards. She is the director of the *Hamaara Itihaas* (*Our History*) archives.

Sahana Ahmed is a fiction writer and poet based in Gurugram. Her work has been published in *The New York Times*, *The Pinch Journal*, and *Flash: The International Short-Short Story Magazine*, among others. *Combat Skirts*, her debut novel, was published by Juggernaut Books. Find her online at www.sahanaahmed.com.

Sambhu R. is a bilingual poet from Kayamkulam. He is working as Assistant Professor of English at N.S.S. College, Pandalam. His poems in English have appeared in *The Bombay Literary Review*, *Madras Courier*, *Borderless Journal*, *Shot Glass Journal*, *The Alipore Post*, *Verse of Silence*, and several others.

Sampurna Chattarji is a writer, translator, editor and teacher with twenty books to her credit. These include her short story collection about Bombay/Mumbai, *Dirty Love* (Penguin, 2013); two novels; and ten poetry titles—the latest being *Elsewhere Where Else* (Poetrywala, 2018) and *Space Gulliver: Chronicles of an Alien* (HarperCollins, 2020).

Sanjeev Sethi has authored five books of poetry. *Wrappings in Bespoke*, his sixth, will be published by The Hedgehog Poetry Press UK. His poems have found a home in over thirty countries in more than 390 journals, anthologies, and online literary venues. He lives in Mumbai. Twitter @sanjeevpoems3 Instagram sanjeevsethipoems

Sanjukta Dasgupta, Professor and Former Head, Dept of English and Former Dean, Faculty of Arts, Calcutta University, is a poet, critic and translator. She is a member of the General Council and Convenor, English Advisory Board of Sahitya Akademi. Her published books of poetry are *Snapshots, Dilemma, First Language, More Light, Lakshmi Unbound, Sita's Sisters, Unbound: New and Selected Poems.*

Sarabjeet Garcha is a poet and translator. He is the author of four books of poems, including *A Clock in the Far Past*, as well as a volume each of translated poetry and translated prose. He has translated several American poets. He is the founder and editorial director of Copper Coin, a multilingual publishing company.

Sarita Jenamani is an India-born Austria-based poet, essayist, literary translator, anthologist, editor of a bilingual magazine for migrant literature — *Words & Worlds* — a human rights activist, a feminist and general secretary of PEN International's Austrian chapter. Her poetry that has so far been published in three collections.

Satya Dash is the recipient of the 2020 Srinivas Rayaprol Poetry Prize and a finalist for the 2020 Broken River Prize. His poems appear in *The Boiler, ANMLY, Waxwing, Rhino Poetry, Cincinnati Review*, and *Diagram*, among others. Apart from having a degree in electronics from BITS Pilani-Goa, he has been a cricket commentator. He grew up in Cuttack and now lives in Bangalore.

Savita Singh is a well-known feminist poet and political theorist. She has four collections of poetry in Hindi, two in

French and two in Odiya; a bilingual collection in Hindi and English. she has received many awards for poetry including Hindi Akademi award, Raza Award, Mahadevi Verma and Eunice de Souza award.

Sayan Aich Bhowmik is currently Assistant Professor, Department of English, Shirakole College. He is the co-editor of *Plato's Caves Online*, a semi academic space of poetry, politics and culture. He has recently brought out his debut collection of poems, *I Will Come With A Lighthouse* (Hawakal Publishers, New Delhi).

Sekhar Banerjee is a poet and a Pushcart Award nominee for 2021. *The Fern-gatherers' Association* (Red River, 2021) is his latest collection of poems. He has been published in *Indian Literature, The Bitter Oleander, Ink Sweat and Tears, Muse India, Bengaluru Review, Kitaab, Better Than Starbucks, The Tiger Moth Review, Thimble Literary Magazine, RIC Journal, Mad in Asia Pacific, Verse Virtual* and elsewhere.

Semeen Ali is the author of four books of poetry and has edited a few poetry anthologies with national and international publishers. She reviews books for leading Indian journals as well as is the Fiction and Poetry editor at *Muse India*.

Shalini Pattabiraman dabbles in writing poetry and haibun. Her work has appeared in anthologies published by Red River Press, Vita Brevis Press and journals like *Wales Haiku, Drifting Sands, O:JAL, The Alipore Post* and *Verse of Silence*. She won the Ken and Noragh Jones Award for Haibun 2021.

Shannan Mann is an Indian-Canadian writer. Her work has appeared or is forthcoming in *Rattle, Rust + Moth, Wildness* and *Amethyst Arsenic*. She was a finalist for the Frontier 2021 Award for New Poets. Her play, *Milkbath*, was selected as the resident production of the Toronto Paprika Theatre Festival.

Shikhandin's books include *After Grief* (Poetry, Red River India), *Impetuous Women* (Penguin-Random House India), *Immoderate Men* (Speaking Tiger), and *Vibhuti Cat* (Duckbill-Penguin-Random House India). She has been widely published in journals and anthologies and has received awards and honours nationally and internationally.

Shikha Malaviya is an Indo-American poet, publisher and mentor. She has been a featured TEDx speaker, two-time Pushcart Prize nominee, and is currently a Mosaic America fellow. Her book of historical persona poetry, *In Her Own Voice: Poems of Anandibai Joshee*, is forthcoming in 2023 from HarperCollins, India. Her previous book of poems is *Geography of Tongues.*

Shilpa Dikshit Thapliyal is an author (*Between Sips of Masala Chai*, Kitaab, 2019) and a Pushcart nominee. Her poems appear in *Quarterly Literary Review Singapore, Yearbook of Indian Poetry in English* 2021, *to let the light in, Atelier of Healing, Shot Glass Journal*, amongst others. Shilpa volunteers at Poetry Festival Singapore.

Shobhana Kumar has two collections of poetry: *The Voices Never Stop* (2012) and **Conditions Apply* (2014), from Writers Workshop, Kolkata. Her work has been anthologised in journals and books of poetry and Japanese short forms.

Siddharth Dasgupta crafts poetry & fiction from lost hometowns and cafés dappled in morning light. His fourth book, *A Moveable East* (Red River), arrived in March '21. Siddharth's literature has appeared in *Epiphany, The Bosphorus Review, Kyoto Journal*, and elsewhere, while he has read in cities around the world.

When Sivakami Velliangiri was Sivakami Ramanathan she published her poems in *Youth Times*, and in various other literary journals. *How We Measured Time* is her debut poetry book. This year, her poems appear in *The Penguin Book of Indian Poets*, edited by Jeet Thayil.

Smita Sahay served as the Associate Editor for the anthology, *Veils, Halos & Shackles: International Poetry on the Oppression and Empowerment of Women*. She is the Editor-in-Chief of the *Usawa Literary Review*, and the Poetry Editor for *SPEAK the Magazine*. She is working on poetry inspired by the coalfields of Jharia, Jharkhand.

Sneha Roy is an independent researcher, writer and speaker. One of the top 30 awardees of the Wingword Poetry Prize 2017, she has been published by *Muse India*, Red River Press, Bangalore Poetry Circle, Indie Blu(e) Publishing, USA and more. She is currently working on a narrative non-fictional piece funded by Zubaan-Sasakawa Peace Foundation Grants.

Sonnet Mondal writes from Kolkata and is the author of *An Afternoon in My Mind* (Copper Coin, 2021), *Karmic Chanting* (Copper Coin, 2018), *Ink and Line* (Dhauli Books, 2018), and five other books of poetry. He serves as the director of Chair Poetry Evenings—Kolkata's International Poetry Festival and managing editor of *Verseville*.

Sonya J. Nair is the editor of Samyukta Poetry. She has been published in *Poetry@Sangam*, *The Book Review*, *Kitchen Sink Magazine*, *EKL Review*, *Borderless Journal*, *The Chakkar*, *INNSAEI*, *Shimmer Spring*, and *Rewriting Human Imagination*, an anthology published by IASE and the Centre for Digital Humanities.

Pushcart Prize nominee Sophia Naz has published in numerous literary journals and anthologies. Her work includes poetry collections *Peripheries*, *Pointillism*, *Date Palms* and *Shehnaz*, a biography. *Open Zero*, her fourth poetry collection, has just been released from Yoda Press. www.SophiaNaz.com

Sridala Swami (poet, fiction writer, children's writer; India) is the author of two poetry collections: *A Reluctant Survivor* (2007) and *Escape Artist* (Aleph Book Company, 2014), and four children's books.

Srividya Sivakumar, a teacher, poet, editor, and TEDx Speaker, has two collections of verse: *The Heart is an Attic*, and *The Blue Note*. She is the co-editor of *The Shape of a Poem—the Red River Anthology of Contemporary Erotic Poetry*. Srividya wrote a weekly column, 'Running on Poetry,' for *The Hindu*'s Metroplus, for eighteen months.

Subhrasankar Das, born on 1st May 1986, hails from Tripura, India. He is an award-winning poet, a translator of distinct repute and a passionate composer. Das authored four books of poems and edits the international (multilingual) video-magazine, *Water*, and the journal, *Shadowkraft*. His verses and prose-pieces have appeared in numerous anthologies, journals and webzines nationally and internationally.

Suchi Govindarajan is a poet, writer and photographer. She's the author of three picture-books for children. Her work has appeared in publications like *Cordite Poetry Review*, *IceFloe Press*, *perhappened magazine* and *Usawa Literary Review*. It's also been included in two anthologies. Poetry is her first love; fiction, her newest.

Sudeep Sen's prize-winning books include *Postmarked India: New & Selected Poems* (HarperCollins), *Rain*, *Aria*, *The*

HarperCollins Book of English Poetry (editor), *Fractals: New &*
Selected Poems | Translations 1980-2015 (London Magazine
Editions), *EroText* (Vintage: Penguin Random House), *Kaifi*
Azmi: Poems | Nazms (Bloomsbury), and *Anthropocene* (Pippa
Rann). www.sudeepsen.org

Sumana Roy is a writer and poet. Her works include *How I*
Became a Tree, a work of non-fiction; *Missing*, a novel; *Out*
of Syllabus, a collection of poems; and *My Mother's Lover and*
Other Stories, a short story collection.

Sumit Shetty is a Pune-based web developer and writer. He's
founded the web portal Webisoda. He is an organizer with
the Pune Writers' Group, and writes short fiction and poetry.
Sumit's work has been published on *The Alipore Post*, *The*
Bombay Literary Magazine, *The Universe Journal*, *Gulmohur*
Quarterly, and *Unlost Journal*.

Tabish Nawaz teaches Environmental Science and Engineering at IIT Bombay. He has published a short-story collection, *Opening Clouds, Fermented Rain* (Hawakal, 2020). His short stories, poems and essays have been published in *nether Quarterly*, *Madras Courier*, *The Bombay Review*, *Woolgathering Review*, *The Punch Magazine*, *Flash Fiction Magazine*, among other venues.

Tasneem Khan is a poet from Lucknow. She is a History student at St. Stephen's College, Delhi. Her work has appeared in the *Monograph Magazine*, *nether Quarterly*, *The Woman Inc*, *Live Wire*, etc. She is a currently working on a poetry manuscript, which she hopes to publish someday.

Teji Sethi, a nutritionist by profession, transitioned from micronutrients to micro poetry. Teji's first book of haiku and senryu, *Moss Laden Walls*, was published in August 2021. She is the founder-editor of a Hindi journal of Haiku, Senryu, Tanka and Micro poems, *TRIYA*.

Tishani Doshi publishes poetry, essays and fiction. For fifteen years she worked as a dancer with the Chandralekha group in Madras. *A God at the Door* is her fourth full-length collection of poems and was shortlisted for the Forward Poetry Prize 2021.

Tuhin Bhowal's poems and translations appear or are forthcoming in *adda* (Commonwealth Writers UK), *Parentheses Journal*, *Ovenbird Poetry*, *Poetry City USA*, *South Florida Poetry Journal*, *Bacopa Literary Review*, *nether*, and elsewhere. He currently serves as a Poetry Editor at *Bengaluru Review*, *Sonic Boom Journal* and Yavanika Press.

Urna Bose is an advertising professional, writer, poet, and editor. As the Deputy Editor for *Different Truths*, she devotes her time to the 'Poet 2 Poet' column.

Usha Akella has authored four books of poetry, one chapbook, and scripted/produced one musical drama. Her latest poetry book is due from Sahitya Akademi. She recently earned 2018 MSt. In Creative Writing at Cambridge University, UK.

Vasvi Kejriwal was born in Kolkata and graduated from the School of Law, Queen Mary University of London. She is a previous winner of the RATTLE Ekphrastic Challenge. Her poems have appeared in *Mekong Review, Dime Show Review, The Alipore Post* and *Radiant Peace Foundation International.*

Vismai Rao's poems appear or are forthcoming in *Salamander, Indianapolis Review, RHINO, Rust + Moth, Glass: A Journal of Poetry, The West Review, Pithead Chapel,* and elsewhere. Her work has been nominated for a Pushcart Prize, Best of the Net, and the Orison Anthology. She serves as Poetry Editor for *The Night Heron Barks.*

Yamini Dand Shah is an academic and editorial advisor, Research Repository (Asian Heritage Foundation), Literature Curator, Core Team (Kala Ghoda Arts Festival), Editor (Paperwall Publishing) and Author of poetry collection, *Abstract Oralism.*

Yashodhara Trivedi works in Delhi as a higher education professional specialising in international projects. She holds an MA in English from Durham University and is a Best of the Net and Pushcart Prize nominee. Her poems have appeared in the *Chestnut Review, The Knight's Library Magazine, The Rising Phoenix Review,* and *The Sunlight Press.*

Zainab Ummer Farook is a poet from Kozhikode. Her poems have been published in *The Bombay Literary Magazine, Narrow Road, nether Quarterly*, and the anthology — *14 International Younger Poets*. She was longlisted for the Toto Funds the Arts [Creative Writing] prize in its 2021 and 2022 editions.

Zeenat Khan is a Delhi-based poet of 21. Her works appear in *Penn Review, Haiku Foundation, Sundress Publication*, Red River, etc. In 2020, she was awarded World Architectural Poetry Award. She is 2022 artist-of-residence in The Seventh Wave. She is an editor at *The Sunflower Collective* and *The Quiver Review*.

Zilka Joseph has authored five collections, the most recent being *In Our Beautiful Bones*. Her books and poems have been nominated, been finalists or won awards for PEN America, Pushcart, Foreword INDIES and Best Indie Book awards. Her writing reflects her Indian and Bene Israel roots, and Western cultures. www.zilkajoseph.com